Dynamic Economic Analysis

Dynamic Economic Analysis

Milton Harris

New York   Oxford
Oxford University Press
1987

Oxford University Press

Oxford   New York   Toronto
Delhi   Bombay   Calcutta   Madras   Karachi
Petaling Jaya   Singapore   Hong Kong   Tokyo
Nairobi   Dar es Salaam   Cape Town

and associated companies in
Beiruit   Berlin   Ibadan   Nicosia

Published by Oxford University Press, Inc.,
200 Madison Avenue, New York, New York 10016

Library of Congress Cataloging-in-Publication Data
Harris, Milton.
Dynamic economic analysis.
Bibliography: p.   Includes index.
1. Equilibrium (Economics)   2. Statics and dynamics (Social sciences)
I. Title.
HB145.H37 1987   339.5   86-23925
ISBN 0-19-504406-1

135798642

Printed in the United States of America
on acid-free paper

*This book is dedicated
to the memory of my mother,
Miriam P. Harris*

Preface

In recent years, a trend has emerged in economic modeling toward incorporating explicit dynamics. For example, asset pricing models in finance, once content to model a single period, have now become explicitly dynamic. In the areas of industrial organization and labor economics, many of the most interesting recent contributions have incorporated explicit dynamics as well as extensive form games. As a result, a number of new tools for analyzing dynamic models have been introduced into the economics literature.

It has now become essential for doctoral students in economics and related fields (e.g. finance and accounting) to become familiar with the tools of dynamic analysis and their applications. This book collects and explains in a detailed, yet understandable, fashion a number of the most widely used techniques in dynamic economic analyses. It is intended to be used as the basis for a one-quarter (ten-week) doctoral course. Of course, by skipping some chapters or sections, one can use the book for a seven-week, half-semester course.

The first chapter introduces some mathematical background with which many economics and finance doctoral students may not be familiar, even those with good mathematical preparation. Thereafter, each chapter covers an important tool used in analyzing dynamic models and presents a significant application. The technique known as "Stationary Discounted Dynamic Programming" is covered in Chapter 2. This approach is then applied to the familiar one-sector optimal growth model. In Chapter 3, the concept of valuation equilibrium is introduced. This concept is applied to the equilibrium version of the one-sector growth model. Chapter 4 is devoted to an exposition of the notion of "Recursive Competitive Equilibrium" and its application to a simple, intertemporal capital assert pricing model. Finally, in Chapter 5, a technique for analyzing extensive form games is presented. This technique, known as sequential equilibrium, is used to develop the celebrated "Revelation Principle."

Each chapter contains exercises that help students sharpen their understanding of the material. A solution manual is available to instructors.

I would like to acknowledge the helpful suggestions of Kerry Back, David Levine, Jong Park, Scott Richard, Jay Shanken, and especially Lars Hansen and Edward C. Prescott. Lynda Borucki carefully proofread the typescript and contributed some of the exercises in Chapter 5.

Evanston, Illinois   M.H.
October 1986

Contents

Chapter 1. Assorted Mathematical Background   3

    1.1. Linear Spaces   3
         Dual Spaces   7
    1.2. Continuity of Solutions to Maximization Problems   8
    1.3. Differentiability   13
    1.4. Representation of Information   14
         Exercises   17
         Notes   17
         References   18

Chapter 2. Stationary Discounted Dynamic Programming   19

    2.1. General Development   20
    2.2. Applications   28
         The One-Sector Growth Model   34
         Exercises   45
         Notes   48
         References   49

Chapter 3. Valuation Equilibrium and Pareto Optimality   50

    3.1. Valuation Equilibrium   51
    3.2. Price Representation of Valuation Equilibria   60
         Infinite Time Horizon   60
         Uncertainty   62

3.3. Application: The One-Sector Equilibrium Model   64
     Pareto Optimality   66
     Valuation Equilibrium   68
     One-Sector Equilibrium Model With Uncertainty   73
     Exercises   82
     Notes   85
     References   87

Chapter 4. Recursive Competitive Equilibrium   89

4.1. General Model   89
4.2. Application and Additional Comment   95
     Heterogeneous Consumer Example   98
     Exercises   103
     Notes   103
     References   104

Chapter 5. Equilibria of Sequential Games   105

5.1. Sequential Equilibrium   105
5.2. Efficient Mechanisms and the "Revelation Principle"   116
     Exercises   127
     Notes   130
     References   131

Index   133

Dynamic Economic Analysis

CHAPTER 1

Assorted Mathematical Background

In this chapter, we introduce several mathematical concepts and results that are used in analyzing dynamic equilibrium problems in economics and finance. Three topics are considered: linear spaces, properties of solutions and value functions of maximization problems, and representation of information by sigma-algebras. It is assumed that the student is familiar with basic topological concepts such as open sets, limits, and continuity in addition to calculus.

1.1 LINEAR SPACES

Since we will be considering economies extending in time over an infinite horizon, or which have an infinite number of "states of the world," or both, we will often be concerned with infinite dimensional commodity spaces. A point in such a space may describe, for example, the quantities of some good delivered (or consumed) at each of an infinite number of dates in the future. That is, points are interpreted as consumption (or production) bundles. We generally require that operations such as adding bundles together and multiplying bundles by scalars (real numbers) be defined. Such operations should result in the creation of new consumption bundles. Sets of points (bundles) with these properties are called "linear." Consequently, we will require some basic familiarity with properties of *linear* spaces (also called "vector spaces"). We start with the definition of a linear space.[1]

Definition 1.1 A *(real)* *vector space* is a set X together with two operations. The first is vector addition which associates with any two elements x and y of X a third element of X denoted $x + y$ (elements of vector spaces are called "vectors"). The second is scalar multiplication (real numbers are called "scalars") which associates with any real number α and any element x of X another element of X denoted αx. The set X and the two operations must satisfy:

1. $x + y = y + x$ (commutativity of vector addition),
2. $(x + y) + z = x + (y + z)$ (associativity of vector addition),
3. There is a null vector 0_X in X such that $x + 0_X = x$ for all $x \in X$,
4. $\alpha(x + y) = \alpha x + \alpha y$,
5. $(\alpha + \beta)x = \alpha x + \beta x$,
6. $(\alpha\beta)x = \alpha(\beta x)$,
7. $0x = 0_X$, $1x = x$.

Generally we will simply use 0 for 0_X whenever the interpretation is clear from the context.

Often it is useful to be able to say how far one vector is from another. There are many ways of measuring distance. For example, on the real line, one could take the distance between two real numbers a and b to be $|a - b|$, or $(a - b)^2$. The following definition describes the properties any distance measure should have (distance for vectors in a linear space is defined in terms of the "norm" of a vector, i.e., its distance from the null vector).

Definition 1.2 If X is any vector space, a *norm* on X is any mapping $\rho : X \to \mathbf{R}$ that satisfies

1. $\rho(x) \geq 0$ for all $x \in X$, $\rho(x) = 0$ if and only if $x = 0_X$,
2. $\rho(x + y) \leq \rho(x) + \rho(y)$ for each $x, y \in X$ (triangle inequality),
3. $\rho(\alpha x) = |\alpha| \rho(x)$ for any real number α and any $x \in X$.

The function ρ is often written $\|\cdot\|$ and $\rho(x)$ is then $\|x\|$. The distance between any two vectors x and y is $\|x - y\|$. A vector space on which a norm is defined is called a *normed linear space*. A property of normed linear spaces which is often useful to assume is completeness:

Definition 1.3 A sequence $\{x^n \mid n = 1, 2, \ldots\}$ in a normed linear space X is *Cauchy* if for any $\varepsilon > 0$, there exists an integer N such that for all $n \geq N$ and $m \geq N$, $\|x^n - x^m\| < \varepsilon$. X is *complete* if every Cauchy sequence in X converges to a point in X. A complete normed linear space is called a *Banach* space.

Example 1.1 $X = \mathbf{R}^n$, for any finite integer n, is a Banach space, where, for x and y in X and α in $\mathbf{R}$

$$x + y = (x_1 + y_1, \ldots, x_n + y_n),$$
$$0_X = (0, \ldots, 0),$$
$$\alpha x = (\alpha x_1, \ldots, \alpha x_n),$$
$$\|x\| = (x_1^2 + \cdots + x_n^2)^{1/2}.$$

This norm is called the *Euclidean* norm and X is called *Euclidean n-Space*.

Example 1.2 Let $E = \{x_1, x_2, \ldots \mid x_t \in \mathbf{R}$ for each $t = 1, 2, \ldots\}$ be the set of real infinite sequences. It is easy to check that E is a vector space under componentwise addition of sequences and componentwise multiplication by scalars (as previously defined for $\mathbf{R}^n$). Define, for $x \in E$,

$$\|x\|_1 = \sum_{t=1}^{\infty} |x_t|,$$

$$\|x\|_p = \left[\sum_{t=1}^{\infty} |x_t|^p \right]^{1/p} \quad \text{for } 2 \leqslant p < \infty, \quad \text{and}$$

$$\|x\|_\infty = \sup_t |x_t|.$$

Also let

$$\ell_p = \{x \in E \mid \|x\|_p < \infty\} \quad \text{for } 1 \leqslant p \leqslant \infty.$$

The norm $\|\cdot\|_\infty$ is called the *sup-norm* on ℓ_∞. It is easy to check that ℓ_p for $1 \leqslant p \leqslant \infty$ are Banach spaces [see Luenberger (1969, pages 29–30, 36–37)]. Note that these norms may also be defined for finite dimensional vector spaces in the obvious way. The norm corresponding to $p = 2$ is the Euclidean norm. In $\mathbf{R}^2$, for example, the unit balls corresponding to the three norms $p = 1, 2, \infty$ are shown in Figure 1.1.

Example 1.3 An example of a normed linear space that is not a Banach space is the following. Let X be the subset of E consisting of those sequences that are zero after a finite number of terms, and let X have the sup-norm. Define the sequence $\{x^n\}$ by

$$x^n = (1, \tfrac{1}{2}, \tfrac{1}{3}, \ldots, 1/n, 0, \ldots).$$

It is easy to check that $\{x^n\}$ is a Cauchy sequence, but, clearly it does not converge to a point in X.

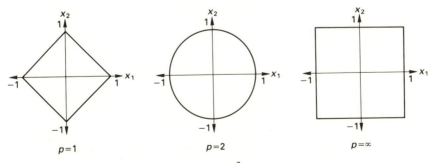

Fig. 1.1 Unit balls in $\mathbf{R}^2$ for $p = 1, 2, \infty$.

Example 1.4   Define the space $L_p[a,b]$, for $p \geq 1$, to consist of those functions x from the interval $[a,b]$ to $\mathbf{R}$ such that $|x|^p$ is Lebesgue integrable. The norm is defined by

$$\|x\|_p = \left[\int_a^b |x(t)|^p \, dt \right]^{1/p},$$

where the integration is Lebesgue integration. Note that $\|x\|_p = 0$ does not imply that $x = 0_X$ since x may be nonzero on a set of measure zero. Therefore, our norm does not satisfy property 1 of Definition 1.2. If, however, we consider two functions x and y to be the same if they differ on at most a set of zero measure (i.e., x and y are the same if $x = y$ amost everywhere or "a.e."), then $L_p[a,b]$ is a normed linear space. Since two functions that are the same almost everywhere will not, in general, have the same supremum, the sup-norm on L_∞ is slightly different from its counterpart on ℓ_∞:

$$\|x\|_\infty = \text{essential supremum} \, |x(t)| = \inf_{y=x \text{ a.e.}} \left\{ \sup_{t \in [a,b]} |y(t)| \right\}.$$

The phrase "essential supremum" is usually abbreviated "ess sup." The L_p spaces are also Banach spaces [see Luenberger (1969, page 37)]. The functions x in $L_p[a,b]$ are often interpreted economically as specifying the amounts of some good to be consumed in various "states of the world"; that is, $x(t)$ is the amount of the good to be consumed if the state of the world is t.

In economic models in which there is a finite number of goods, we are usually interested in equilibrium prices of these goods. These prices can be used to calculate the value of a commodity bundle as the inner product of the price vector and the bundle. This inner product is a linear function: the value of the sum of two commodity bundles is the sum of their values. The generalization of this notion to economies with an infinite number of commodities is that a price system is a linear functional on the commodity space.

Definition 1.4   A _functional_ on a linear space X is any mapping $f: X \to \mathbf{R}$. A _linear functional_ f on X is a functional that satisfies

$$f(\alpha x + \beta y) = \alpha f(x) + \beta f(y), \quad \text{for any} \quad \alpha, \beta, \in \mathbf{R}, \quad \text{and} \quad x, y \in X.$$

Example 1.5   Let $X = \mathbf{R}^n$. Any function of the form

$$f(x) = \sum_{k=1}^n a_k x_k = a \cdot x,$$

whre $x = (x_1, \ldots, x_n)$ and $a = (a_1, \ldots, a_n) \in \mathbf{R}^n$ is a linear functional on X. Moreover, _any_ linear functional f on $X = \mathbf{R}^n$ can be represented by a point $a \in \mathbf{R}^n$ such that, for any $x \in X$, $f(x) = a \cdot x$ [see Exercise 1.1]. Thus the set of linear functionals on $\mathbf{R}^n$ can be identified with $\mathbf{R}^n$ itself.

Definition 1.5 A linear functional f on a normed linear space X is *bounded* if there is a real number $M < \infty$ such that $|f(x)| \leq M \|x\|$ for all $x \in X$ (where $\|\cdot\|$ is the given norm on X). The smallest such M is called the *norm* of f, denoted $\|f\|$.

An equivalent definition of the norm of f is,

$$\|f\| = \sup_{\|x\|=1} |f(x)|.$$

To see this, let M be the norm of f. Let $S = \sup\{|f(x)| \mid \|x\| = 1\}$. By definition of the norm of f, $M \geq S$. Let $x \in X$ be arbitrary. If $x = 0$, then $|f(x)| = 0 = S \|x\|$ [otherwise, for any $y, f(y) = f(y + 0) = f(y) + f(0) \neq f(y)$]. If $x \neq 0$, let $\alpha = 1/\|x\|$ and let $y = \alpha x$. Then $\|y\| = 1$, so

$$S \geq |f(y)| = |f(\alpha x)| = |\alpha| |f(x)| = |f(x)|/\|x\| \quad \text{or} \quad |f(x)| \leq S \|x\|.$$

Since x is arbitrary, we have shown that $|f(x)| \leq S \|x\|$ for all $x \in X$. Since M is the smallest such number $M \leq S$. Since we have both $M \leq S$ and $M \geq S$, we conclude that $M = S$.

Dual spaces

Having defined linear functionals, we now wish to consider spaces of such functionals. The space of linear functionals on a space X is called the dual space of X. Since a price system will be an element of the dual space of our commodity space, it is useful to record some basic properties of dual spaces.

Let X be a normed linear space. Define vector addition and scalar multiplication of linear functionals on X by

$$(f_1 + f_2)(x) = f_1(x) + f_2(x),$$
$$(\alpha f)(x) = \alpha[f(x)].$$

With these definitions, it is easy to show that the set of linear functionals on X is a vector space. It is also easy to verify that the space of all bounded linear functionals on X is a normed linear space (with the above defined norm). This space is called the *normed dual* (or just *dual*) of X, denoted X^*.

Example 1.6 Let X be Euclidean n-space. Then $X^* = X$. [Most of the proof is contained in Example 1.5 and Exercises 1.1 and 1.2. For more detail, see Luenberger (1969, page 107).]

Example 1.7 The dual of ℓ_1 is ℓ_∞ [Luenberger (1969, Theorem 1, page 107)].

Example 1.8   The dual of ℓ_∞ contains ℓ_1 but does not equal ℓ_1. This fact plays an important role in Chapter 3. There we consider an economic model in which the commodity space is ℓ_∞. Since the dual of ℓ_∞ is not ℓ_1, we cannot, in general, conclude that the equilibrium price system for this model can be represented as a sequence of prices.

One more result will be useful:

Lemma 1.1   A linear functional on a normed linear space X is continuous (with respect to the topology on X determined by the norm on X) if and only if it is bounded.

Thus the dual of a normed linear space X may also be described as the space of continuous linear functionals on X.

1.2 CONTINUITY OF SOLUTIONS TO MAXIMIZATION PROBLEMS

We will often need to be able to show that the maximized value of the objective function and the solution to a maximization problem are continuous in certain parameters appearing in the problem. In this section, we present some results that can be used for this purpose.[2]

First we define two concepts of continuity for set-valued mappings. In this section, let X and Y be topological spaces, 2^Y be the power set of Y (i.e., the set of subsets of Y), Γ be a (set-valued) mapping of X into 2^Y, and x_0 be a point in X.

Definition 1.6 Γ is *lower hemi-continuous* (*LHC*) at x_0 if for every open set G such that $G \cap \Gamma(x_0) \neq \varnothing$, there exists a neighborhood $U(x_0)$ such that $x \in U(x_0)$ implies $G \cap \Gamma(x) \neq \varnothing$.

Definition 1.7 Γ is *upper hemi-continuous* (*UHC*) at x_0 if for every open set G such that $\Gamma(x_0) \subset G$, there exists a neighborhood $U(x_0)$ such that $x \in U(x_0)$ implies $\Gamma(x) \subset G$.

Definition 1.8 Γ is LHC on X if it is LHC at each $x \in X$.

Definition 1.9 Γ is said to have *closed graph* if it is UHC at each $x \in X$. If, in addition, $\Gamma(x)$ is compact for every $x \in X$, then Γ is UHC on X.

Definition 1.10   If Γ is LHC and UHC on X then Γ is *continuous* on X.

The following examples will provide some intuition for these definitions. Let X and Y be two intervals in $\mathbf{R}$. In Figures 1.2–1.5, the graph of Γ is the shaded region, including the boundary.

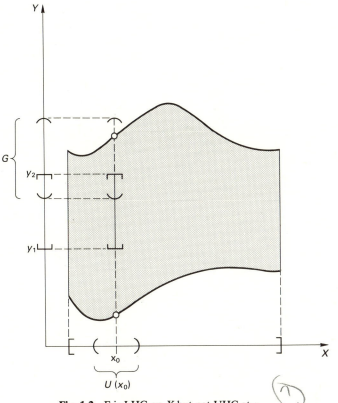

Fig. 1.2 Γ is LHC on X but not UHC at x_0.

Example 1.9 In Figure 1.2, $\Gamma(x_0)$ is the interval $[y_1, y_2]$. Γ is LHC on X but not UHC at x_0.

Example 1.10 In Figure 1.3, $\Gamma(x_0)$ is the interval $[y_3, y_4]$. Γ is UHC on X but not LHC at x_0.

Example 1.11

$$\Gamma(x) = \begin{cases} [0,1], & x \in X \quad \text{and} \quad x \neq x_0, \\ \{1\}, & x = x_0. \end{cases}$$

Γ is LHC at every $x \in X$ but not UHC at x_0. Γ is UHC at every $x \in X$, $x \neq x_0$ [see Figure 1.4].

Example 1.12

$$\Gamma(x) = \begin{cases} [0,1], & x \in X \quad \text{and} \quad x \neq x_0, \\ [0,2], & x = x_0. \end{cases}$$

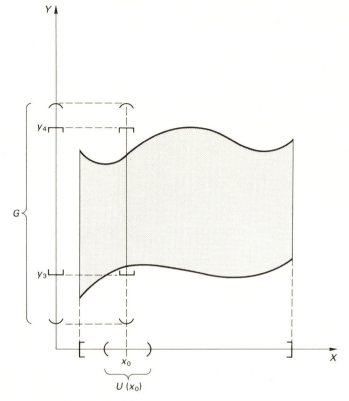

Fig. 1.3 Γ is UHC on X but not LHC at x_0.

$\Gamma(x)$ is UHC at every $x \in X$, but not LHC at x_0. $\Gamma(x)$ is LHC at every $x \in X$, $x \neq x_0$ [see Figure 1.5].

The results we will need in the sequel are as follows.

Lemma 1.2 Suppose Γ is UHC on X and for every $x \in X$, $\Gamma(x)$ is a singleton. Then the function defined by Γ is continuous on X.

Proof By Berge (1963, Theorem 2, page 110), Γ UHC on X implies that for every open set $G \subset Y$, the set $\{x \in X \mid \Gamma(x) \subset G\}$ is open. By Kolmogorov and Fomin (1970, Theorem 10, page 87), a mapping $\Gamma : X \to Y$ is continuous if the pre-image, $\Gamma^{-1}(G)$, of every open set $G \subset Y$ is open (this is usually taken as the definition of continuity). Since Γ is singleton-valued,

$$\Gamma^{-1}(G) = \{x \subset X \mid \Gamma(x) \subset G\} = \{x \subset X \mid \Gamma(x) \subset G\}. \qquad \text{Q.E.D.}$$

While $\Gamma(x) = \{y\}$ is not a function because it maps points in X into single-element subsets of Y, there is an obvious, analogous function

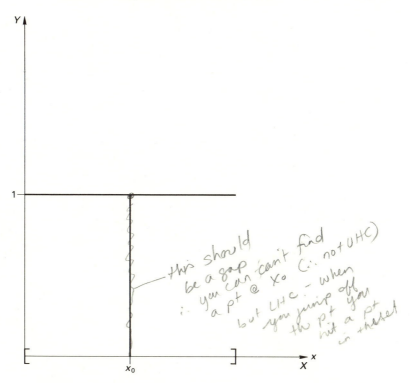

Fig. 1.4 Γ is LHC on X but not UHC at x_0.

$\gamma(x) = y$. Here we use the same notation, Γ, for both types of mappings. Which type of mapping is being referred to will be clear from the context.

Theorem 1.1 If $\phi : X \times Y \to \mathbf{R}$ is continuous on $X \times Y$, if Γ is continuous on X and if $\Gamma(x) \neq \varnothing$ for every $x \in X$, then $M : X \to \mathbf{R}$ defined by

$$M(x) = \max_{y \in \Gamma(x)} \phi(x,y)$$

is continuous on X, and the set of maximizers

$$\Phi(x) = \operatorname*{argmax}_{y \in \Gamma(x)} \phi(x,y) = \{y \in Y \mid y \in \Gamma(x), \ \phi(x,y) = M(x)\}$$

is UHC on X. Furthermore, if Φ is a singleton for every $x \in X$, then $\Phi : X \to Y$ is continuous on X.

Proof This is essentially the "Maximum Theorem" [Berge (1963, page 116)] except that we allow ϕ to depend on x as well as y. It is clear that if ϕ is continuous on $X \times Y$, then the proof given in Berge goes through with

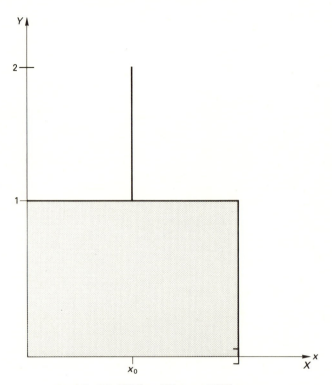

Fig. 1.5　Γ is UHC on X but not LHC at x_0.

obvious modification. The last statement of the Theorem follows from Lemma 1.2.

Q.E.D.

Two useful results for checking continuity of correspondences are:

Lemma 1.3　If $f:X \times Y \rightarrow \mathbf{R}$ is continuous on $X \times Y$ and if Y is compact, then the mapping $\Gamma:X \rightarrow 2^Y$ defined by $\Gamma(x) = \{y \in Y \mid f(x,y) \leq 0\}$ is UHC on X.[3]

Proof　This follows from the example, Berge (1963, page 111), which shows that Γ is a closed mapping or that the graph of Γ is a closed set, and the corollary, Berge (1963, page 112).

Theorem 1.2　Suppose $f:X \rightarrow Y$ is continuous on X and Y is a compact subset of $\mathbf{R}$. Define $\Gamma:X \rightarrow 2^Y$ by $\Gamma(x) = \{y \in Y \mid y \leq f(x)\}$. Then Γ is continuous on X.

Proof　The strategy for this proof is to use Lemma 1.3 to establish that Γ

is UHC on X and then to use the continuity of f to show that Γ is LHC on X. Then since Γ is UHC and LHC on X, Γ is continuous on X.

To show Γ is UHC on X, Γ can be rewritten as $\Gamma(x) = \{y \in Y \mid y - f(x) \leq 0\}$ to satisfy the hypotheses of Lemma 1.3. Since $f(x)$ is continuous, $y - f(x)$ is continuous. Y is compact. Therefore, by Lemma 1.3, $\Gamma(x)$ is UHC on X.

To show Γ is LHC on X, we show that for every $x_0 \in X$, Γ is LHC at x_0. Let G be an open subset of Y such that $G \cap \Gamma(x_0) \neq \varnothing$. We need to find a neighborhood $U(x_0)$ such that $x \in U(x_0)$ implies $\Gamma(x) \cap G \neq \varnothing$. By the continuity of f, for every $\varepsilon > 0$, there exists $U(x_0)$ such that $x \in U(x_0)$ implies $|f(x) - f(x_0)| < \varepsilon$. We consider two cases.

Case 1. There exists a $y_0 \in G \cap \Gamma(x_0)$ such that $y_0 < f(x_0)$.

Let $\varepsilon = f(x_0) - y_0 > 0$. Then there exists a $U(x_0)$ such that $x \in U(x_0)$ implies $|f(x) - f(x_0)| < \varepsilon$. This implies that for every $x \in U(x_0)$, $-\varepsilon + f(x_0) < f(x)$. Thus, for every $x \in U(x_0)$, $y_0 < f(x)$, by the construction of ε. Then $y_0 \in \Gamma(x)$, by definition of $\Gamma(x)$. Since $y_0 \in G$, by assumption, $y_0 \in \Gamma(x) \cap G$. Therefore, $\Gamma(x) \cap G \neq \varnothing$.

Case 2. There does not exist a $y_0 \in \Gamma(x_0) \cap G$ such that $y_0 < f(x_0)$.

If there does not exist such a y_0, then $\Gamma(x_0) \cap G = \{f(x_0)\}$. Since $f(x_0) \in G$ and since G is an open subset of Y, there exists an $\varepsilon > 0$ such that for any $y \in Y$, if $|y - f(x_0)| < \varepsilon$, then $y \in G$. Since f is continuous, let $U(x_0)$ be such that

$$|f(x) - f(x_0)| < \varepsilon$$

for all $x \in U(x_0)$. Thus for all $x \in U(x_0)$, $f(x) \in G$ by choice of ε. But, by definition of Γ, $f(x) \in \Gamma(x)$ for all x. Thus, for any $x \in U(x_0)$,

$$f(x) \in \Gamma(x) \cap G \neq \varnothing. \qquad \text{Q.E.D.}$$

1.3 DIFFERENTIABILITY

Here we state a simple lemma that will be useful in proving the differentiability of certain functions which arise in dynamic programming. The proof may be found in Benveniste and Scheinkman (1979).

Lemma 1.4 Suppose $V^* : D \to \mathbf{R}$, where $D \subseteq \mathbf{R}^n$ and V^* is concave over any convex subset of D. Suppose $x_0 \in$ interior of D and $V : D \to \mathbf{R}$ is:

1. concave in a neighborhood of x_0,
2. differentiable at x_0,
3. $V(x_0) = V^*(x_0)$,
4. $V(x) \leq V^*(x)$ for every x in a neighborhood of x_0.

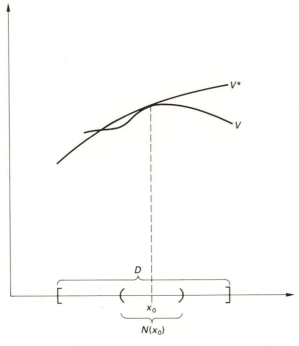

Fig. 1.6   Differentiability.

Then V^* is differentiable at x_0 and $\nabla V^*(x_0) = \nabla V(x_0)$, where ∇ indicates the gradient operator.

The lemma can be motivated by Figure 1.6 (for the case $n = 1$). Note that there is no way that V^* can have a kink or discontinuity at x_0 given the hypotheses of the lemma.

1.4 REPRESENTATION OF INFORMATION

In economic models involving uncertainty that is resolved over time, we must have a formal way of specifying what economic agents know at various points in time. A simple and elegant method is to represent their information as a collection of events that it is possible for them to distinguish. For example, it may be possible to distinguish the event that the Allies won World War II at any time after 1945 but not before 1945. Such a collection should have certain properties in order to be interpreted as a collection of discernible events. For example, if we can tell that the event that the Allies won World War II did occur, then surely we can tell that the event that the Allies lost did not occur. Similarly, if we can tell that the events "it rained last Monday" and "it rained last Tuesday" occurred, then we should be able to tell that the joint event "it rained last Monday and Tuesday" occurred. Collections of events which satisfy these (and one other) properties are called "algebras of events." More formally,

Definition 1.11   Let Ω be any set. We interpret Ω as the set of "elementary events" or "states of the world." A subset of Ω is interpreted as an "event." A nonempty collection $\mathcal{A}$ of subsets of Ω is called an *algebra* if $\mathcal{A}$ is closed under union, intersection, and complementation, that is,

If A and B are elements of $\mathcal{A}$, then so are A^c, $A \cup B$, and $A \cap B$.

Note that Definition 1.11 implies that if $\mathcal{A}$ is an algebra, then both Ω and $\emptyset$ are discernible events.

Definition 1.12   An algebra $\mathcal{A}$ is a *σ-algebra* if it is closed under countable unions, that is,

$$\text{If } \{A_n \mid n = 1, 2, \ldots\} \subset \mathcal{A}, \quad \text{then } \bigcup_{n=1}^{\infty} A_n \in \mathcal{A}.$$

It is easy to show, using DeMorgan's Laws, that a σ-algebra is closed under countable intersections (see Exercise 1.4).

Often we start with a set of events that is not a σ-algebra and wish to expand it into one. Consequently, we will need some notation for this operation. If Ψ is any collection of events, let

$\sigma(\Psi)$ be the smallest σ-algebra that contains Ψ.

We refer to $\sigma(\Psi)$ as the σ-algebra *generated by* Ψ.

Example 1.13   If T is a topology on Ω—that is, T is the collection of open subsets of Ω—then $B(\Omega) = \sigma(T)$ is called the family of *Borel* subsets of Ψ. Thus $B(\Omega)$ includes all open sets, closed sets, and intersections of these sets.

Example 1.14   Suppose $\Omega = \{1,2,3\}$, and $P_1 = \{\{1\}, \{2\}, \{3\}\}$. Note that P_1 is called a *partition* of Ω because the three sets in P_1 have empty intersections with each other and their union equals Ω. The σ-algebra generated by P_1 is simply the set of all subsets of Ω. This is the finest σ-algebra of subsets of Ω. If one's information is represented by $\sigma(P_1)$, then one knows exactly which state of the world occurred. Note that the σ-algebra generated by $P_2 = \{\{1,2\}, \{2,3\}\}$ is exactly the same as that generated by P_1. This makes sense, because, for example, if one can tell that the state of the world is either 1 or 2 and also that it is either 2 or 3, then surely one knows that the state is 2.

The evolution of information over time—that is, the "information structure"—of an economy can easily be modeled using σ-algebras.

Example 1.15 Let $\Omega = \Lambda \times \Lambda$, where Λ is a finite set. We can interpret the two components of the state of the world $\omega = (\lambda_1, \lambda_2)$ as the state at dates 1 and 2, respectively. Assuming the state at date 1 is observable at date 1, but the state at date 2 is observable only at date 2, then the information structure (assuming complete recall) can be represented by the two σ-algebras $\sigma(P_1)$ and $\sigma(P_2)$, where P_1 consists of subsets of Ω of the form $\{\lambda_1\} \times \Lambda$ and P_2 consists of subsets of the form $\{\lambda_1\} \times \{\lambda_2\}$, for $\lambda_1, \lambda_2 \in \Lambda$.

When the model consists of an infinite number of dates, we generally model the state of the world as being an infinite-dimensional vector whose first t components are observable at date t. Formally let $\Omega = \Lambda \times \Lambda \times \ldots$, where $\Lambda \subset \mathbf{R}^m$, that is, $\omega \in \Omega$ is an infinite sequence $\{\lambda_t\}$ of m-dimensional real vectors. Then we denote by Φ the σ-algebra consisting of all eventually discernible events. That is, Φ is the σ-algebra of subsets of Ω generated by all sets of the form $\prod_{t=1}^{\infty} A_t$, where A_t is a Borel subset of Λ for each t and $A_t = \Lambda$ for all but a finite number of values of t (such sets are called *cylinder sets*—see Example 1.15 above for a finite example). Thus an event might be something like

$$\lambda_1 = 2, \quad \lambda_2 = 5, \quad \lambda_3 \in [0,3], \quad \lambda_4 = 0, \quad \lambda_t \in \Lambda \quad \text{for } t > 4.$$

That is, an event is a subset of Ω such that, after some finite amount of time, one can tell whether or not ω is in that subset. Similarly, Φ_t will be the σ-algebra of subsets of Ω generated by all sets of the form $\prod_{s=1}^{\infty} A_s$, where A_s is a Borel subset of Λ for each s and $A_s = \Lambda$ for all $s > t$. This simply means that one can observe the history of the process, but one cannot observe at date t components occurring after date t.

A function $z : \Omega \to \mathbf{R}$ is a random variable. Such a function might describe, for example, how much of a certain good is to be delivered in each state of the world. Note that by observing the realization of z, one can infer something about which state of the world has occurred—that is, the random variable z contains information. It is often useful to assume that z does not convey more information than is represented by a certain σ-algebra. Formally, we say that z is "measurable" with respect to the given σ-algebra. The definition of measurability is as follows.

Definition 1.13 A random variable z is *measurable* with respect to a σ-algebra Φ (or z is Φ-measurable) if $\{\omega \in \Omega \mid z(\omega) \leq a\} \in \Phi$ for any $a \in \mathbf{R}$. If $\mathcal{F} = \{\Phi_t \mid t = 1, 2, \ldots\}$ is a sequence of σ-algebras in Φ such that $\Phi_t \subset \Phi_{t+1}$, then $\mathcal{F}$ is called a *filtration* of Ω. If $z = \{z_t\}$ is a sequence of random variables such that z_t is Φ_t-measurable for every t, then z is said to be *adapted* to the filtration $\mathcal{F}$.

Note that filtrations represent information which is increasing over time, since its σ-algebras are increasing in size over time. It can be shown (see Exercise 1.5) that if $\mathcal{F}$ is the filtration generated by observing the history of the state of the world process, and if z is adapted to $\mathcal{F}$, then, for each t, z_t can depend on at most the first t components of ω.

EXERCISES

1.1. Show that any linear functional f on $\mathbf{R}^n$ can be represented by a point $a \in \mathbf{R}^n$ such that, for any $x \in \mathbf{R}^n$, $f(x) = a \cdot x$. *Hint*: choose $a_k = f(0, 0, \ldots, 0, 1, 0, \ldots, 0)$ where the one is in the kth place.

1.2. Let $X = \mathbf{R}^n$ with the usual Euclidean norm. Show that, for any linear functional f on X, $\|f\|$ is the Euclidean norm of the point in $\mathbf{R}^n$ corresponding to f (see Example 1.5). Note, this is shown on page 107 of Luenberger (1969) using the Cauchy–Schwartz inequality. For this exercise show it using the Lagrange multiplier technique to solve the maximization problem in Definition 1.5 (you may assume that the problem has a solution).

1.3. Let X be $\mathbf{R}^n$ with the sup-norm. Show that $X^* = \mathbf{R}^n$ with the ℓ_1 norm.

1.4. Show that any σ-algebra is closed under countable intersections.

1.5. Assume that the filtration $\mathcal{F}$ is generated by the history of the ω-process. Prove that if the random variable z is Φ_t-measurable, then z can depend on at most the first t components of ω.

NOTES

1. This section is based primarily on Luenberger (1969, Chapter 2).
2. This section is based primarily on Berge (1963). Debreu (1959, Chapter 1) also covers this material. Debreu's definitions of continuity of correspondences are somewhat different from Berge's, as the following example (due to Keuk Je Sung) will show: Let $X = \mathbf{R}$, $Y = [1,2]$, $Q =$ set of rationals in Y, $Q' = Y - Q$, x_0 be any irrational number, and

$$\Gamma(x) = \begin{cases} Q & \text{if } x \text{ is rational} \\ Q' & \text{if } x \text{ is irrational and } x \neq x_0 \\ Q' \cup \{1,2\} & \text{if } x = x_0. \end{cases}$$

According to Berge Γ is both LHC and UHC at x_0, but according to Debreu Γ is LHC but not UHC at x_0.
3. That Γ may not be LHC on X is shown by the following example (also due to Keuk Je Sung): Let $X = [0,1]$, $Y = [a,b]$, where $0 < a < \frac{1}{2} < b < 1$, and

$$f(x,y) = \begin{cases} x/2(1-y) & \text{if } \frac{1}{2} \leq y \leq b, \\ (2y + x - 1)/2y & \text{if } a \leq y \leq \frac{1}{2}. \end{cases}$$

It can be shown that $\Gamma(0) = [0,1]$ and $\Gamma(x) = [0,(1-x)/2]$ for $x > 0$. Thus Γ is UHC for all x but not LHC at 0.

REFERENCES

Berge, C., *Topological Spaces* (New York: Macmillan, 1963).

Benveniste, L. M. and J. A. Scheinkman, "On the Differentiability of the Value Function in Dynamic Models of Economics," *Econometrica*, **47,** 3 (May 1979), pp. 727–732.

Debreu, G., *Theory of Value* (New York: Wiley, 1959).

Kolmogorov, A. N. and S. V. Fomin, *Introductory Real Analysis* (New York: Dover, 1970).

Luenberger, D. G., *Optimization by Vector Space Methods* (New York: Wiley, 1969).

CHAPTER 2

Stationary Discounted Dynamic Programming

To analyze dynamic equilibrium models, we must first be able to characterize solutions to dynamic optimization problems since the behavior of agents in these models will be determined by the solutions to such problems. Consequently, in this chapter, we consider a technique for solving dynamic optimization problems that fall into a particular class called "stationary discounted dynamic programming" problems. This is a class for which excellent analytical techniques exist, and often agents can be modeled as solving problems in the class. The techniques developed here can be used both for characterizing the properties of solutions analytically and for calculating numerical solutions. Both uses are illustrated in this chapter. An example of such a problem is

$$(P) \quad \max \sum_{t=1}^{\infty} \beta^{t-1} u(c_t)$$

subject to

$$k_{t+1} \leq f(k_t) + (1 - \delta)k_t - c_t = F(k_t) - c_t \quad \text{for } t = 1, 2, \ldots$$
$$c_t \geq 0, \quad k_t \geq 0 \quad \text{for } t = 1, 2, \ldots$$
$$k_1 = \bar{k} \quad \text{given} \quad (\bar{k} > 0)$$

where the maximization is over all infinite sequences $\{k_t, c_t\}$. Here c_t and k_t are real numbers, β and δ are parameters with $0 < \beta < 1$ and $0 < \delta < 1$, f is a concave, real-valued function and u is a bounded, continuous real-valued function. One may interpret a solution of this problem as the optimal path of capital accumulation and consumption in a one-good economy. Here $u(c)$ would be the utility of an "economic planner" for current consumption c,

$$\sum_{t=1}^{\infty} \beta^{t-1} u(c_t)$$

is his utility for the infinite stream $\{c_t\}$ of consumption, $f(k)$ is the amount of the single good that can be produced from a stock of the good of size k, δ is the depreciation rate of the good, and $\bar{k}$ is the historically given initial stock of the good. To lighten the notation, we shall generally denote net output, $f(k) + (1 - \delta)k$, by $F(k)$. This example is the standard, neoclassical, one-sector growth model.[1] It, or some modification of it, forms the basis for many models in macroeconomics and asset pricing. We shall characterize its solution in detail in this chapter.

First we develop some general tools, then we apply these to economic problems.

2.1 GENERAL DEVELOPMENT

Out first task in learning how to solve dynamic optimization problems is to describe formally the class of problems to be dealt with. This is a fairly large class of problems often labeled stationary discounted dynamic programming problems (the reason for the adjectives stationary and discounted will become clear in the discussion).[2] The class includes both stochastic problems and nonstochastic problems.

Formally, a problem consists of five objects:

1. S, the set of possible "states of the system" at any time. S is any nonempty Borel set in a finite dimensional Euclidean space.
2. $D(s)$, a correspondence that associates with each state s a nonempty set $D(s)$. The set $D(s)$ is interpreted as the set of *feasible decisions* if the state is s. We denote $\bigcup_{s \in S} D(s)$ by A.
3. q, the "law of motion" of the system. q is a conditional probability on S given $S \times A$, that is, $q(s' | s, a)$ is the cumulative conditional probability that the next state is $\leq s'$ given that the current state is s and the current decision is a. Note that the law of motion is assumed to be a first-order Markov process. Also, q may be degenerate.
4. r, the one-period return function. r is a real-valued, bounded function on $S \times A$. We interpret $r(s, a)$ as the current return (or income or utility) if the current state is s and the current action is a.
5. β, the discount factor, $0 < \beta < 1$.

Note that r is assumed to be bounded. By this is meant that

$$\sup_{(s,a)\in S \times A} |r(s,a)| < \infty.[3]$$

For this chapter, we will define the norm of any real-valued function f defined on some set X by

$$\|f\| = \sup_{x \in X} |f(x)|.$$

Thus in this notation, r bounded means $\|r\| < \infty$. Note that this norm is different from the one used for linear functionals in Chapter 1. Actually, all that is required is that the operator U used in defining the optimality equation (see below) is well defined and has a unique fixed point. Boundedness of r is a sufficient, but not a necessary condition for U to satisfy these properties.

A (feasible) *policy*, or *decision rule*, for a stationary discounted dynamic programming problem is a mapping $\pi : S \to A$ such that $\pi(s) \in D(s)$ for each $s \in S$. Thus a policy is a choice of a feasible decision as a function of the state. Denote by Π the set of all policies. Any policy π, along with the law of motion q, defines a distribution on all possible futures of the system $(a_1, s_2, a_2, \ldots)$ conditional on any given initial state s_1. Here a_t refers to the action or decision taken at time t and s_t refers to the state of the system at time t for $t = 1, 2, \ldots$. We denote this conditional distribution by e_π, that is, $e_\pi(a_1, s_2, a_2, \ldots \mid s_1)$ is the conditional probability that the future of the system will be $(a_1, s_2, a_2, \ldots)$, given that the initial state is s_1. Associated with any policy π is a *value*

$$I(\pi)(s) = E_\pi \left\{ \sum_{n=1}^{\infty} \beta^{n-1} r(s_n, a_n) \mid s_1 = s \right\}$$

interpreted as the expected total discounted return from the policy π starting from an initial state $s_1 = s$. The expectation E_π is taken with respect to the distribution e_π. The problem then is to find a policy $\pi \in \Pi$ such that $I(\pi) \geqslant I(\pi')$ for every $\pi' \in \Pi$. The notation $I(\pi) \geqslant I(\pi')$ means $I(\pi)(s) \geqslant I(\pi')(s)$ for every $s \in S$. Some sufficient conditions on r and q that guarantee this problem is well defined are now developed.

We start by examining an equation which plays a key role in the solution technique. This equation is variously referred to as "the optimality equation" (by Blackwell), "the functional equation," and "Bellman's equation."

Let $M(S)$ denote the set of bounded functions mapping the state space S into $\mathbf{R}$. For any policy π, define the operator T_π mapping $M(S)$ into itself by

$$(T_\pi u)(s) = r(s, \pi(s)) + \beta \int_S u(s') \, dq(s' \mid s, \pi(s)), \quad \text{for any } u \in M(S).$$

Clearly $(T_\pi u) : S \to \mathbf{R}$ for any $u \in M(S)$ and $(T_\pi u)$ is bounded since r and u are bounded. We may interpret $(T_\pi u)(s)$ as the value starting from state s of choosing action $\pi(s)$ today then terminating tomorrow with receipt of $u(s')$ as a function of tomorrow's state, s'. If $u = I(\pi')$ for some policy π', then we may interpret $(T_\pi u)(s)$ as the value starting from s of choosing action $\pi(s)$ today then following policy π', starting tomorrow.

The following four lemmas will be useful.

Lemma 2.1 $M(S)$ is complete.

Proof   Suppose $\{u_n\}$ is a Cauchy sequence in $M(S)$. Since, for each $s \in S$, $\{u_n(s)\}$ is a Cauchy sequence in **R** and **R** is complete (in the usual metric, i.e., absolute value), $u_n(s)$ converges to a point, say $u(s)$ in **R**. Thus $u : S \rightarrow \mathbf{R}$. Let $\varepsilon > 0$ be given. Choose N such that $\|u_n - u_m\| < \varepsilon/2$, for any $n, m \geq N$. Now for any $n \geq N$ and $s \in S$,

$$|u_n(s) - u(s)| \leq |u_n(s) - u_m(s)| + |u_m(s) - u(s)|$$
$$\leq \|u_n - u_m\| + |u_m(s) - u(s)|.$$

By choosing m sufficiently large (which may depend on s), each term on the right can be made smaller than $\varepsilon/2$. Thus, for any s, $|u_n(s) - u(s)| < \varepsilon$.

To see that u is bounded, we have

$$\|u\| \leq \|u - u_n\| + \|u_n\| \quad \text{for any } n.$$

Since $\|u_n - u\| \rightarrow 0$ and $u_n \in M(S)$ we can choose n sufficiently large that the right-hand side is finite.   Q.E.D.

Lemma 2.2   For any $\pi \in \Pi$, T_π is monotone, that is, if u, $v \in M(S)$ with $u \geq v$, then $T_\pi u \geq T_\pi v$.

Proof   See Exercise 2.1.

Before proceeding we must define the important concept of a contraction mapping which is used repeatedly in the sequel. The basic idea of a contraction mapping is that, given any two points, it maps these two points into two new points which are closer together than the original points. The formal definition is as follows.

Definition 2.1   A mapping F from a set X with distance measure d into itself is a contraction of modulus β if for any two points x and y in X,

$$d[F(x), F(y)] \leq \beta d(x, y).$$

Lemma 2.3   If $U : M(S) \rightarrow M(S)$ is monotone and for some $0 < \beta < 1$, $U(u + c) \leq Uu + \beta c$, where c is any constant function, then U is a contraction of modulus β.

Proof   This proof is due to Blackwell (1965). Let v and u be any two functions in $M(S)$. Then $v - u \leq \|u - v\|$, or $v \leq u + \|u - v\|$. Therefore, using the two properties assumed for U, we have

$$Uv \leq Uu + \beta \|u - v\|$$

or

$$Uu - Uv \geq -\beta \|u - v\| \quad \text{for any } s \in S.$$

Since $u - v \leqslant \|u - v\|$, the above argument can be repeated to obtain

$$Uu - Uv \leqslant \beta \|u - v\| \quad \text{for any } s.$$

These two inequalities imply that

$$|Uu - Uv| \leqslant \beta \|u - v\| \quad \text{for any } s$$

or

$$\|Uu - Uv\| \leqslant \beta \|u - v\|. \qquad \qquad \text{Q.E.D.}$$

Lemma 2.4 For any $\pi \in \Pi$, T_π is a contraction mapping of modulus β.

Proof The result follows immediately from Exercise 2.2 (following), Lemma 2.2, and Lemma 2.3.   Q.E.D.

Next we introduce an operator $U : M(S) \rightarrow M(S)$ defined by

$$(Uu)(s) = \sup_{a \in D(s)} r(s,a) + \beta \int_S u(s') \, dq(s' \mid s,a).$$

Clearly Uu is bounded.

Theorem 2.1 U is a contraction mapping of modulus β.

Proof This proof is due to Denardo (1967, p. 176). Let u and v be arbitrary elements of $M(S)$ and s be an element of S. Let $k = (Uu)(s) - (Uv)(s)$, and first suppose that $k \geqslant 0$. By definition of U, for each positive integer n, we can choose a policy π_n such that

$$(T_{\pi_n} u)(s) \geqslant (Uu)(s) - k/n.$$

Also, by definition of U and k, we have

$$(Uu)(s) - k/n \geqslant (Uv)(s) \geqslant (T_{\pi_n} v)(s).$$

Combining these three inequalities gives

$$0 \leqslant (Uu)(s) - (Uv)(s) - k/n \leqslant (T_{\pi_n} u)(s) - (T_{\pi_n} v)(s)$$
$$\leqslant \beta \|u - v\|,$$

for each n. Taking limits as n approaches infinity implies that

$$|(Uu)(s) - (Uv)(s)| \leqslant \beta \|u - v\|.$$

This inequality is similarly established for the case of $k < 0$. Since u, v, and s are arbitrary, this completes the proof.   Q.E.D.

We can interpret $(Uu)(s)$ as the value starting from state s of choosing an optimal action today given that the process terminates tommorow with the receipt of $u(s')$ as a function of tomorrow's state, s'. Note that "optimal" takes account of the influence of a on s'. If $u(s')$ is the value of following some policy π starting from state s', that is, if $u(s') \equiv I(\pi)(s')$, then $(Uu)(s)$ can be interpreted as the value of choosing an optimal action today given that the policy π will be followed starting tomorrow.

A function $u^* \in M(S)$ is said to satisfy the *optimality equation* if

$$u^* \equiv Uu^* \quad \text{for each } s \in S, \tag{2.1}$$

that is, u^* satisfies (2.1) if and only if it is a fixed point of U. Note that if u^* satisfies (2.1), then the value of choosing the best action today given that, starting tomorrow, you will follow a plan whose value is u^* is equivalent to just following the plan starting today. It turns out that, if we can find a solution to (2.1), it will then be relatively easy to find an optimal plan, as is shown in Theorem 2.3, below.

The following two theorems will provide a method for "solving" the type of problems discussed in this chapter.

Theorem 2.2 U has a unique fixed point u^*, that is, (2.1) has a unique solution. Moreover, if u is any function in $M(S)$,

$$U^* = \lim_{n \to \infty} U^n u,$$

where $U^n u$ is the result of applying U to u, n times.

Proof This is essentially the Banach or "Contraction Mapping" fixed point theorem [see, e.g., Kolmogorov and Fomin (1970, Theorem 1, page 66)]. Choose u in $M(S)$ and let

$$u_n = U^n u \quad \text{for } n = 1, 2, \dots.$$

We first show that $\{u_n\}$ is a Cauchy sequence in $M(S)$. Suppose $n \leq m$. Then

$$\begin{aligned}
\|u_n - u_m\| = \|U^n u - U^m u\| &= \|U^n u - U^n(U^{m-n}u)\| \\
&\leq \beta^n \|u - u_{m-n}\| \quad \text{by Theorem 2.1} \\
&\leq \beta^n[\|u - u_1\| + \|u_1 - u_2\| + \cdots + \|u_{m-n-1} - u_{m-n}\|] \\
&\leq \beta^n[1 + \beta + \cdots + \beta^{m-n-1}] \|u - u_1\| \\
&< \beta^n \|u - u_1\|/(1 - \beta).
\end{aligned}$$

Since $\beta < 1$ and $u - u_1$ is bounded, this shows that $\{u_n\}$ is Cauchy. Since $M(S)$ is complete (Lemma 2.1), u_n converges to, say, u^* in $M(S)$. Since U is a contraction (Theorem 2.1), U is continuous, so

$$Uu^* = \lim_{n \to \infty} Uu_n = \lim_{n \to \infty} u_{n+1} = u^*.$$

This proves that u^* is a fixed point of U and that u^* can be obtained as the limit of a sequence of functions that results from repeatedly applying U to some element u of $M(S)$. To see that u^* is unique, if v is also a fixed point of U, we have, from the definition of a contraction,

$$\|u^* - v\| \leq \beta \|u^* - v\|.$$

This implies, however, that $u^* = v$ since $\beta < 1$. Since there is only one fixed point of U, and we previously showed that, for any u in $M(S)$, $U^n u$ converges to a fixed point, $U^n u$ must converge to u^*. \hfill Q.E.D.

This result shows that the optimality equation always has a unique solution and provides a way of computing such a solution. The importance of solutions to (2.1) is given in Theorem 2.3 below. First some notation. Let

$$I^*(s) = \sup_{\pi \in \Pi} I(\pi)(s).$$

Thus I^* is the *optimal return function*. Our objective is to find I^* and a policy π that achieves I^*.

Theorem 2.3 Let u^* be the unique solution of (2.1). Then $u^* = I^*$. Further, suppose that for each s, $\pi^*(s)$ solves

$$\sup_{a \in D(s)} r(s,a) + \beta \int_S u^*(s')\, dq(s' \mid s,a). \tag{2.2}$$

Then $I(\pi^*) = u^* = I^*$ and so π^* is an optimal policy.

Proof First we claim that, for any policy π, $I(\pi)$ is a fixed point of T_π. This is intuitively obvious since $T_\pi I(\pi)$ is the value of using policy π today then receiving tomorrow the value of using π forever starting tomorrow. This is simply the value of using π forever starting today, that is, $I(\pi)$. Note that since T_π is a contraction (Lemma 2.4), the proof of Theorem 2.2 shows that T_π has a unique fixed point and (since $I(\pi)$ is a fixed point as just argued),

$$T_\pi^n u \to I(\pi)$$

for any u in $M(S)$.

Second we claim that for any u in $M(S)$ and policy π,

$$\|I(\pi) - u\| \leq \|T_\pi u - u\|/(1 - \beta).$$

To see this, from the triangle inequality and since T_π is a contraction, we have (assuming $T_\pi^0 u = u$),

$$\|T_\pi^n u - u\| \leq \sum_{i=1}^{n} \|T_\pi^i u - T_\pi^{i-1} u\|$$

$$\leq \sum_{i=1}^{n} \beta^{i-1} \|T_\pi u - u\| \leq \|T_\pi u - u\|/(1 - \beta).$$

The claim now follows by taking limits of both sides and using the first claim above.

Third we claim that for any $\varepsilon > 0$, there is a policy π such that $\|I(\pi) - u^*\| \leqslant \varepsilon$ [this is proved as Corollary 1, page 167 of Denardo (1967)]. To see this, note that by definition of U, there exists a policy π such that

$$\|T_\pi u^* - U u^*\| \leqslant \varepsilon(1 - \beta).$$

This claim now follows from the previous one and the fact that u^* is the fixed point of U.

We may now argue that $u^* \leqslant I^*$, for if not, by the third claim, if $u^*(s) > I^*(s)$ for some s, we could find a policy π such that $I(\pi)(s) > I^*(s)$. This contradicts the definition of I^*. To show the opposite inequality, note that by definition of U and the fact that u^* is the fixed point of U, we have

$$T_\pi u^* \leqslant U u^* = u^*.$$

Therefore, by monotonicity of T_π,

$$T_\pi^2 u^* \leqslant T_\pi u^* \leqslant U u^* = u^*.$$

Repeating this argument implies that

$$T_\pi^n u^* \leqslant u^* \quad \text{for any } n.$$

But, from above, taking limits of both sides implies that $I(\pi) \leqslant u^*$. Since this is true for every policy π, we have shown that $I^* \leqslant u^*$. Combined with the previous inequality, this establishes that $I^* = u^*$.

To prove the second part, note that since π^* solves (2.2) and u^* solves (2.1) and $I^* = u^*$,

$$T_{\pi^*} I^* = T_{\pi^*} u^* = U u^* = u^* = I^*.$$

Therefore, I^* is a fixed point of T_{π^*}. But, from above, $I(\pi^*)$ is the unique fixed point of T_{π^*}. Consequently, $I^* = I(\pi^*)$.   Q.E.D.

The following corollaries give some sufficient conditions for (2.2) to have a solution.

Corollary 2.1 Suppose for some topology on S and A, r is continuous on $S \times A$ and $D(s)$ is continuous as a correspondence on S. Also suppose that

For any bounded continuous function f on S,
$\int f(s') \, dq(s' \mid s,a)$ is continuous as a function of (s,a).   (2.3)

Then (2.2) has a solution. If the solution is unique, it is continuous on S.

Proof First we show that under (2.3), U maps bounded continuous functions into bounded continuous functions. Clearly if $r(s,a) + \beta \int_S u(s') \, dq(s' \mid s,a)$ is continuous on $S \times A$ for any bounded continuous u, then we may apply Theorem 1.1 to conclude that Uu is continuous.

That $r + \beta \int_S u \, dq$ is continuous on $S \times A$ is guaranteed by (2.3) and continuity of r on $S \times A$.

Now since U maps bounded continuous functions into bounded continuous functions, we may conclude that the solution u^* of (2.1) is continuous. Consequently, by (2.3) and the assumption that r is continuous, the objective function of (2.2) is continuous. Since $D(s)$ is assumed to be compact, (2.2) has a solution. Also note from Theorem 1.1, the set of solutions is upper hemi-continuous in s and if the solution of (2.2) is unique, it is a continuous function on S.

Corollary 2.2 Suppose $q(s' \mid s,a)$ is degenerate on $s' = \xi(s,a)$, where $\xi : S \times A \to S$ is continuous on $S \times A$. Then q satisfies (2.3) and if the other hypotheses of Corollary 2.1 are satisfied, the conclusion of Corollary 2.1 holds.

Proof See Exercise 2.3.

There is one more general result that will be useful in simplifying dynamic programming problems. Suppose we have two problems, (Q) and (Q') defined, respectively, by S, $D(\cdot)$, r, q, β and S', $D'(\cdot)$, r', q', β'. Further suppose that the problems are related as follows:

1. $S' = \bigcup_{s \in S} E_s$, where $\{E_s\}_{s \in S}$ is a collection of nonempty, pairwise disjoint subsets of S', that is, each point in S corresponds to a set of points in S'. For example, suppose the state variable in Q' is (t,x), where t is an integer (the "date") and x is a real number (e.g., the capital stock) while the state variable in Q is just x. For any $x \in S$, let $E_x = \{(t,x) \mid t \in N\}$.
2. $D'(s') = D(s)$ for each $s' \in E_s$ and $s \in S$, that is, the constraint set depends only on s. In the above example, the constraint set in Q' must depend only on x and not on t.
3. For each $s \in S$, $a \in D(s)$, $s' \in E_s$, and $u \in M(S)$,

$$r'(s',a) + \beta' \int_{S'} h_u(z) \, dq'(z \mid s',a) = r(s,a) + \beta \int_S u(z) \, dq(z \mid s,a),$$

where h_u is defined by

$$h_u(s') = u(s) \quad \text{for any } s' \in E_s.$$

Note that $h_u \in M(S')$. This assumption states that the objective function of the maximization problem in the optimality equation of Q' depends only on s.
4. $\beta' = \beta$.

In this case, problem (Q') is said to be *generated from problem* (Q). It turns out that (Q) and (Q') are equivalent in the following sense.

Theorem 2.4 Let (Q') be generated from (Q) and suppose (Q) has optimal value function u^*. Then h_{u^*} is the optimal value function of (Q') and if π^* is an optimal policy for (Q), then $w(\pi^*)$ is an optimal policy for (Q'), where $w(\pi^*)(s') = \pi^*(s)$ for any $s' \in E_s$ and each $s \in S$.

Proof This is just Theorem 5, page 172 of Denardo, specialized to the present model.

2.2 APPLICATIONS

Before returning to the one-sector optimal growth problem (P) given at the beginning of this chapter, it is useful to consider a somewhat simpler example. This problem has the advantage that numerical solutions can easily be generated using commercially available computer software.

Consider a product that can be produced using either of two machines. A type y machine will last y years $(y = 1, 2)$ and costs K_y to purchase, with $K_1 < K_2$. Either machine can produce as many units of the product per period as desired at a cost of q^2, where q is output in the period. The firm that produces this product takes its price in each period as given. This price is assumed to follow a Markov chain on the two states H (for high) and L (for low), that is, if $\bar{p}_t$ is the (random) price in period t, then

$$\Pr(\bar{p}_{t+1} = H \mid \bar{p}_t = H) = \pi_1,$$
$$\Pr(\bar{p}_{t+1} = L \mid \bar{p}_t = L) = \pi_2.$$

Finally, to make things simpler, we assume that the firm may have only one machine in any period, purchases of machines may be made after observing the price of output in that period, and that no sales of machines are allowed. (The problem is not intended to be realistic; it is intended only to illustrate the solution techniques considered in this chapter.) The firm seeks to choose its output q_t and its purchases of each type of machine, m_{yt} for $y = 1, 2$, in each period $t = 1, 2, \ldots$ so as to maximize the expected present value of profits, given by

$$E \sum_{t=1}^{\infty} \beta^t [p_t q_t - q_t^2 - m_{1t} K_1 - m_{2t} K_2],$$

where β is a discount factor strictly between 0 and 1, subject to the constraints previously mentioned.

Our first task in analyzing this problem is to formulate it as a stationary discounted dynamic programming problem. To do this, we must specify the state variables (and their domain, the state space S), the set of feasible decisions for each state $(D(s)$ for each s in $S)$, the law of motion of the state and the one-period return function, r.

Generally, the most difficult aspect of the formulation is specifying the state variables. The basic idea in this choice is that the state variables must summarize all the information obtained by observing past realizations of exogeneous random variables and decisions that is relevant for making current decisions. Moreover, the analysis will be simpler if the smallest such set of variables is chosen. For the problem at hand, in order to choose current output and purchases of machines, the firm must know how many machines it has inherited from the past (all of these will be type 2 machines; the type 1 machines purchased in the past will have been scrapped). In addition, all information about future prices is summarized by the current price, because the price process is Markovian. Since this information is relevant both for choosing today's output and any machine purchases, we want to include current price in our list of state variables. As there are no other variables that contain decision-relevant information, we may take our state space to be

$$S = \{0,1\} \times \{H,L\},$$

where we interpret the first component of the state vector, s_1, as the number of type 2 machines inherited from the past (this number can only be 0 or 1) and the second component, s_2, as the current price (either H or L).

The constraint on the number of machines which can be purchased in any period is given formally by

$$s_1 + m_1 + m_2 \leq 1. \tag{2.4}$$

Since it turns out that we can eliminate current output as a choice variable from the formulation (following), we will specify the decision correspondence, $D(s)$, as the set of feasible choices of m_1 and m_2 given the state s:

$$D(s) = \{(m_1,m_2) \in \{0,1\}^2 \mid (2.4) \text{ holds}\}.$$

The law of motion for the state is simplified by the fact that next period's price distribution does not depend on the number of machines inherited from the past (s_1) or on this period's decision. Also the number of machines available next period depends only on how many type 2 machines are purchased this period. Thus the law of motion can be expressed as

$$s_1' = m_2,$$
$$\Pr(s_2' = H \mid s_2 = H) = \pi_1,$$
$$\mathrm{pr}(s_2' = L \mid s_2 = L) = \pi_2,$$

where s' denotes next period's state. It is important to notice that current output, q, does not affect next period's state. This enables us to eliminate it from the formulation.

Given output q and purchases of machines m_y, $y = 1, 2$, the one-period payoff to the firm is

$$s_2 q - q^2 - m_1 K_1 - m_2 K_2.$$

Although we could use this function as our one-period return function r in the formulation, it is possible to simplify the formulation by noticing that when we perform the optimization in the optimality equation (2.1), q appears only in the term involving the current payoff. In particular, as noted above, q does not appear in the law of motion, and hence does not affect future payoffs or constraints. Therefore, choosing an optimal current output is really a static problem in this example. We can choose q to maximize the above expression, then substitute the optimal value into the expression to obtain our one-period return function r. Since the optimal q is easily seen to be $s_2/2$ (provided we have one machine, i.e., $s_1 + m_1 + m_2 = 1$), we may choose

$$r(s,m) = \begin{cases} s_2^2/4 - m_1 K_1 - m_2 K_2 & \text{if } s_1 + m_1 + m_2 = 1, \\ 0 - m_1 K_1 - m_2 K_2 & \text{if } s_1 + m_1 + m_2 = 0. \end{cases}$$

To state the optimality equation for this problem, first observe that if one (type 2) machine is inherited from the past, then the firm cannot purchase a machine in the current period $(m_1 = m_2 = 0)$, and, consequently, it will begin next period with no machines $(s_1' = 0)$. Therefore, if $s_1 = 1$, we have that the value function u^* must satisfy

$$u^*(1, s_2) = s_2^2/4 + \beta E[u^*(0, s_2') \mid s_2],$$

where the expectation is taken using the probabilities π_1 and π_2 given in the law of motion. On the other hand, if no machines are inherited from the past, the firm may choose to purchase no machines $[m = (0,0)]$, one type 1 machine $[m = (1,0)]$, or one type 2 machine $[m = (0,1)]$. The payoffs corresponding to these decisions are

$$\begin{aligned}
P(0,0) &= 0 + \beta E[u^*(0, s_2') \mid s_2] & \text{if } m = (0,0), \\
P(1,0) &= s_2^2/4 - K_1 + \beta E[u^*(0, s_2') \mid s_2] & \text{if } m = (1,0), \\
P(0,1) &= s_2^2/4 - K_2 + \beta E[u^*(1, s_2') \mid s_2] & \text{if } m = (0,1).
\end{aligned}$$

Therefore, the value function, when $s_1 = 0$, must satisfy

$$u^*(0, s_2) = \max\{P(m) \mid m = (0,0), (1,0), (0,1)\}.$$

This completes the formulation of the example.

Because the state space S contains only four elements, this problem can be solved as a system of four equations in the four unknowns $u^*(0, H)$, $u^*(0, L)$, $u^*(1, H)$, and $u^*(1, L)$. Since two of the equations are nonlinear (involving the "max operator"), this is somewhat tedious to do analytically and will not be pursued here. Instead, we will show how to solve the problem numerically using a spreadhseet program such as Lotus $1-2-3^4$. Before proceeding, let's simplify the problem a bit further by assuming that

$$H^2/4 > K_2 \qquad (2.5)$$

and

$$L^2/4 < K_1. \qquad (2.6)$$

Assumption (2.5), along with $K_1 < K_2$, rules out $m = (0,0)$ as a solution when $s_2 = H$. Assumption (2.6) rules out $m = (1,0)$ when $s_2 = L$. These two assumptions leave us the following optimality equations:

$$u^*(1,H) = H^2/4 + \beta[u^*(0,H)\pi_1 + u^*(0,L)(1 - \pi_1)], \qquad (2.7)$$

$$u^*(1,L) = L^2/4 + \beta[u^*(0,H)(1 - \pi_2) + u^*(0,L)\pi_2], \qquad (2.8)$$

$$u^*(0,H) = \max[P(1,0), P(0,1)], \qquad (2.9)$$

$$u^*(0,L) = \max[P(0,0), P(0,1)]. \qquad (2.10)$$

The basic idea for solving this problem (or any dynamic programming problem) numerically, is to use the iterative technique, given in Theorem 2.2, for approximating the solution to the optimality equation. More specifically, one may begin with any function, $u_0(s)$; $u_0 \equiv 0$ is the usual choice. One then substitutes this function into the right-hand side of the optimality equation and calculates a new function u_1. This procedure is repeated until the changes $\|u_{n+1} - u_n\|$ are "sufficiently small" (how small is sufficient depends on the application).

Implementing this procedure using a spreadsheet program such as $1-2-3$ is especially easy.[5] To do this, one inserts formulas into the cells of row $n + 2$ that calculate the values of u_n using the numbers calculated in row $n + 1$ as the values of u_{n-1}. It is a good idea to use row 1 of the spreadsheet for column headings. The values for u_0 are then entered into row 2, and so on. This can most easily be accomplished by entering the formulas for u_1 into row 3 using *relative* cell addresses for the values of u_0 in row 2. These formulas, when copied into subsequent rows, will automatically be updated by the spreadsheet program to use the values of u found in the previous row (references to cells containing parameter values such as β should use absolute addresses). The procedure is started by entering numerical values for u_0 (usually zeroes) into the cells of row 2.

One particular implementation of the foregoing procedure for the example at hand is shown in Table 2.1. The first column, A, is used to keep track of the iteration number, n, corresponding to each row. Columns B and C contain formulas for calculating $u_n(0,H)$ and $u_n(0,L)$, respectively, while columns D and E contain formulas for $u_n(1,H)$ and $u_n(1,L)$, respectively. The formula for $u_n(0,H)$ requires finding the larger of two numbers $P(1,0)$ and $P(0,1)$. These numbers are calculated in the

Table 2.1 Numerical Analysis of Durability Example

	A	B	C	D	E	F	G	H	I
1	N	U0H	U0L	U1H	U1L	P(1,0)	P(0,1)	P(0,0)	P(0,1)
2	0	0.00	0.00	0.00	0.00				
3	1	1.25	0.00	2.25	0.25	1.25	0.75	0.00	−1.25
4	2	2.07	0.60	2.95	0.85	1.95	2.07	0.60	−0.09
5	3	2.61	1.19	3.55	1.44	2.55	2.61	1.19	0.44
6	4	3.08	1.63	3.99	1.88	2.99	3.08	1.63	0.91
7	5	3.44	2.00	4.37	2.25	3.37	3.44	2.00	1.27
8	6	3.74	2.29	4.66	2.54	3.66	3.74	2.29	1.57
9	7	3.97	2.53	4.89	2.78	3.89	3.97	2.53	1.80
10	8	4.16	2.71	5.08	2.96	4.08	4.16	2.71	1.99
11	9	4.30	2.86	5.23	3.11	4.23	4.30	2.86	2.14
12	10	4.43	2.98	5.35	3.23	4.35	4.43	2.98	2.26
13	11	4.52	3.08	5.44	3.33	4.44	4.52	3.08	2.35
14	12	4.60	3.15	5.52	3.40	4.52	4.60	3.15	2.43
15	13	4.66	3.22	5.58	3.47	4.58	4.66	3.22	2.49
16	14	4.71	3.27	5.63	3.52	4.63	4.71	3.27	2.54
17	15	4.75	3.30	5.67	3.55	4.67	4.75	3.30	2.58
18	16	4.78	3.34	5.70	3.59	4.70	4.78	3.34	2.61
19	17	4.80	3.36	5.73	3.61	4.73	4.80	3.36	2.63
20	18	4.82	3.38	5.75	3.63	4.75	4.82	3.38	2.65
21	19	4.84	3.40	5.76	3.65	4.76	4.84	3.40	2.67
22	20	4.85	3.41	5.78	3.66	4.78	4.85	3.41	2.68
23	21	4.86	3.42	5.79	3.67	4.79	4.86	3.42	2.69
24	22	4.87	3.43	5.79	3.68	4.79	4.87	3.43	2.70
25	23	4.88	3.44	5.80	3.69	4.80	4.88	3.44	2.71
26	24	4.88	3.44	5.81	3.69	4.81	4.88	3.44	2.71
27	25	4.89	3.44	5.81	3.69	4.81	4.89	3.44	2.72
28	26	4.89	3.45	5.81	3.70	4.81	4.89	3.45	2.72
29	27	4.89	3.45	5.82	3.70	4.82	4.89	3.45	2.72
30	28	4.90	3.45	5.82	3.70	4.82	4.90	3.45	2.73
31	29	4.90	3.45	5.82	3.70	4.82	4.90	3.45	2.73
32	30	4.90	3.46	5.82	3.71	4.82	4.90	3.46	2.73
33	31	4.90	3.46	5.82	3.71	4.82	4.90	3.46	2.73
34	32	4.90	3.46	5.82	3.71	4.82	4.90	3.46	2.73
35	33	4.90	3.46	5.82	3.71	4.82	4.90	3.46	2.73
36	34	4.90	3.46	5.82	3.71	4.82	4.90	3.46	2.73
37	35	4.90	3.46	5.83	3.71	4.83	4.90	3.46	2.73

	K	L	M	N	O
1	BETA	0.8		H	3.0
2	KAY1	1.0		L	1.0
3	KAY2	1.5		PIE1	0.7
4				PIE2	0.4

Cell	Formula
B3	@MAX(P10P01)
C3	@MAX(P00P01)
D3	+$H*$H/4 + $BETA*($PIE1*U0H +(1 − $PIE1)*U0L)
E3	+$L*$L/4 + $BETA*($PIE2*U0L +(1 − $PIE2)*U0H)
F3	+$H*$H/4 − $KAY1 + $BETA*($PIE1*U0H +(1 − $PIE1)*U0L)
G3	+$H*$H/4 − $KAY2 + $BETA*($PIE1*U1H +(1 − $PIE1)*U1L)
H3	+$BETA*($PIE2*U0L + (1 − $PIE2)*U0H)
I3	+$L*$L/4 − $KAY2 + $BETA*($PIE2*U1H +(1 − $PIE2)*U1L)

Range	Range Name
B2	U0H
C2	U0L
D2	U1H
E2	U1L
F3 ·· G3	P10P01
H3 ·· I3	P00P01
L1	BETA
L2	KAY1
L3	KAY2
O1	H
O2	L
O3	PIE1
O4	PIE2

corresponding row of columns F and G. This range of cells in row 3 is given the range name P10P01 and the formula in cell B3 (see p. 2 of Table 2.1) uses this range name as a relative address so that when the formula is copied into subsequent cells, the maximization range will correspond to the cells in columns F and G of the current row. Meanwhile, the formulas for $P(1,0)$ and $P(0,1)$ in cells F3 and G3, respectively (see p. 2 of Table 2.1), use the range names U0H, U0L, U1H, and U1L, which correspond to cells B2, C2, D2, and E2, respectively. These cells contain the initial values of u_0, namely, zeroes. The formula for $u_n(0,L)$ requires finding the larger of the two numbers $P(0,0)$ and $P(0,1)$. These numbers are calculated in the corresponding row of columns H and I. This range of cells in row 3 is given the range name P00P01 and this name is used in the same way as P10P01. Similarly, the formulas for $P(0,0)$ and $P(0,1)$ in row 3 use the range names U0H, U0L, U1H, and U1L. All of these formulas are simply copied into rows 4 through 37. At row 37, or iteration 35, u_n has converged to two decimal places, which was taken to be sufficient for this application.

Note that, instead of using numerical values in the formulas for the parameters β, K_1, K_2, H, L, π_1 and π_2, these values were stored in cells named BETA, KAY1, KAY2, H, L, PIE1, and PIE2, respectively. The absolute addresses of these cells (indicated by a dollar sign, $, in front of their names) were used in the formulas. This procedure facilitates experimentation with various parameter values.

The solution can be read from row 37. The value of an optimal policy if the current price is high ($s_2 = H$) and one has no working machines ($s_1 = 0$), U0H, is 4.90. This corresponds to the payoff associated with purchasing a type 2 machine, $P(0,1)$, in column G. Consequently, one should purchase a type 2 machine in this situation. If the current price is low ($s_2 = L$), the value of the optimal policy is 3.46 corresponding to the payoff associated with purchasing no machines, $P(0,0)$, in column H. Therefore, one should not purchase any machines in this situation. Of course, if $s_1 = 1$, one has no choice. The optimal output was found above to be the current price divided by 2.

Finally, note that one can interpret the "solution" at iteration n to be the solution of the finite horizon problem with n periods to go, given that the problem terminates with receipt of u_0. Thus, for example, the solution of the two period problem is found in row 4 (in this case, the optimal policy is the same for problems of all horizons). Moreover, the numerical values of u_n give the value to the firm of being in various states.

The one-sector growth model

Let us now return to the one-sector optimal growth problem (P) given at the beginning of this chapter and restated here for convenience:

$$(P) \max \sum_{t=1}^{\infty} \beta^{t-1} u(c_t)$$

subject to

$$k_{t+1} \leq f(k_t) + (1 - \delta)k_t - c_t = F(k_t) - c_t \quad \text{for } t = 1, 2, \ldots$$
$$c_t \geq 0, \qquad k_t \geq 0 \qquad \qquad \text{for } t = 1, 2, \ldots$$
$$k_1 = \bar{k}, \quad \text{given } (\bar{k} > 0)$$

where the maximization is over all infinite sequences $\{k_t, c_t\}$. Recall that c_t is interpreted as the amount of the single good consumed at date t, k_t is the amount used for production (i.e., the "capital stock") at date t, $F(k_t)$ is the total output plus undepreciated capital, and u is the period utility of a planner.

We must first show that this problem is indeed a stationary discounted dynamic programming problem. To see this we will first need some assumptions on the functions u and f of (P).

Assumption 2.1

1. f is strictly monotone increasing, twice continuously differentiable and strictly concave on $\mathbf{R}_+$ and for some $0 < \hat{k} < \infty$, $f(\hat{k}) = \delta\hat{k}$. Note that $\hat{k}$ is the largest capital stock that can be maintained. It follows that $f(k) > \delta k$ for $k < \hat{k}$ and $f(k) < \delta k$ for $k > \hat{k}$. It also follows that $f(k) - \delta k$ reaches a maximum, say m, at some $0 < k_m < \hat{k}$ (and $f'(k_m) = \delta$). Net additions to capital are maximized at k_m. (See Figure 2.1.)
2. u is twice continuously differentiable, strictly concave and strictly increasing on $\mathbf{R}_+$.

Note that we do not need to assume that u is bounded because the set of feasible consumption levels will be shown to be compact and we are assuming that u is continuous.

We may now prove some preliminary results.

Lemma 2.5 If $\{k_t, c_t\}$ is any feasible path for (P), then $0 \le k_t \le B$ and $0 \le c_t \le B + m$, where $B = \max(\hat{k} + m, \bar{k})$.

Proof Obviously $0 \le k_t$ and $0 \le c_t$ by assumption. It is easy to show, using Assumption 2.1.1, that if $k_t > \hat{k}$, then $k_{t+1} < k_t$. Also note that, for any t, $k_{t+1} \le k_t + m$. The proof that $k_t \le B$ is by induction on t. Clearly

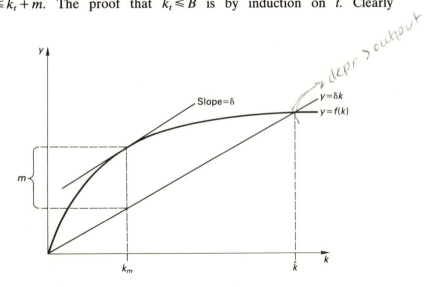

Fig. 2.1 Production technology for the one-sector model.

$k_1 = \bar{k} \le B$. Suppose $k_t \le B$. We must show that this implies $k_{t+1} \le B$. But if $k_t \le \hat{k}$, then $k_{t+1} \le k_t + m \le \hat{k} + m \le B$. If $k_t > \hat{k}$, then $k_{t+1} < k_t \le B$ by the induction hypothesis. This establishes the claim. Now

$$0 \le c_t \le F(k_t) \le m + B \quad \text{for every } t. \qquad \text{Q.E.D.}$$

Lemma 2.6 The inequality constraints *= you'll never throw any away*

$$k_{t+1} \le F(k_t) - c_t, \quad t = 1, 2, \ldots$$

must hold as equalities at any solution to (P).

Proof Suppose for some T we have

$$k_{T+1} < F(k_T) - c_T.$$

Consider the path $\{k_t', c_t'\}$, which is identical to $\{k_t, c_t\}$ except that we replace c_T by

$$c_T' = F(k_T) - k_{T+1} > c_T.$$

The new path is feasible and yields higher value of the objective function (since $u(c_T') > u(c_T)$ by Assumption 2.1.2 and $u(c_t') = u(c_t)$ for $t \ne T$) than $\{t_t, c_t\}$. Thus $\{k_t, c_t\}$ cannot be a solution. \qquad Q.E.D.

These two lemmas together imply that (P) may be replaced by the equivalent problem

$$\max_{\{c_t, k_t\}} \sum_{t=1}^{\infty} \beta^{t-1} u(c_t)$$

subject to

$$k_{t+1} = F(k_t) - c_t \quad \text{for all } t,$$
$$c_t \in [0, m+B] \quad \text{for all } t,$$
$$k_t \in [0, B] \qquad \text{for all } t,$$
$$k_1 = \bar{k}.$$

Henceforth (P) will refer to the foregoing problem. To see that (P) may be formulated as previously outlined, let

amt. of k at t = 0

$$S = [0, B] \times N, \text{— } nat. \#s (time)$$

$$D(k,t) = \{c \in [0, m+B] \mid c \le F(k)\} \quad \text{for any } (k, t) \in S,$$

$$A = [0, m+B], \qquad s - old(?) . amt of consmpt.$$

q assign probability 1 to $(k', t') = (F(k) - a, t + 1)$ and 0 to any other state, given current state (k, t) and action a, and

$$r(k, t, a) = u(a),$$

where $N = \{1, 2, \ldots\}$. Notice that D and r do not depend explicitly on t. Also q is degenerate. For any function $g(k,t)$, the notation $\int g(k',t') \, dq(k',t' \mid k,t,a)$ simply means $g[F(k) - a, t + 1]$.

Any (feasible) policy for this problem describes a feasible path for (P), that is, if π is a policy, let

$$c_t = \pi(k_t, t),$$
$$k_{t+1} = F(k_t) - \pi(k_t, t) \quad \text{for each } t,$$
$$k_1 = \bar{k}.$$

Lemma 2.7 If π^* is an optimal policy for the dynamic programming problem, then the corresponding path solves (P).

Proof See Exercise 2.4.

Thus to solve (P) it suffices to solve the associated dynamic programming problem previously described.

Finally, note that r is continuous on $S \times A$ (since u is continuous on A and r doesn't depend on k and t) and A is compact so that r is bounded on $S \times A$.

We now apply the above results to problem (P) previously described. We will consider the equivalent dynamic programming formulation which we will now call problem (Q') defined by

$$S' = [0, B] \times N,$$
$$D'(s,t) = \{c \in [0, m + B] \mid c \leq F(s)\} \quad \text{for } (s,t) \in S',$$
$$A' = [0, m + B],$$

q' assigns probability 1 to $(s', t') = (F(s) - c, t + 1)$ and 0 to any other state, given current state (s, t) and action c, and

$$r'(s,t,c) = u(c) \quad \text{for } (s,t) \in S', \; c \in A'.$$

The reason for using prime notation is that we will use Theorem 2.4 to eliminate t as a state variable. Thus the above problem, labeled (Q') corresponds to problem (Q') in Theorem 2.4. We obtain problem (Q) by dropping t as a state variable.

Consider problem (Q) defined by

$$S = [0, B],$$
$$D(s) = \{c \in [0, m + B] \mid c \leq F(s)\} \quad \text{for } s \in S,$$
$$A = [0, m + B],$$

q assigns probability 1 to $s' = F(s) - c$ and 0 to any other state, given current state s and action c, and

$$r(s,c) = u(c)$$

and with discount factor β the same as in (Q'). We claim that (Q') is generated from (Q). To see this let

$$E_s = \{(z,t) \in S' \mid z = s\} = \{s\} \times N \quad \text{for } s \in S.$$

It is easy to check that the sets E_s are nonempty and pairwise disjoint and that their union is S' (see Exercise 2.5).

Now clearly

$$D'(s,t) = D(s) \quad \text{for every } s \in S.$$

For any $v \in M(S)$,

$$h_v(s,t) = v(s).$$

Thus for any $s \in S$, $c \in D(s)$, $(s,t) \in E_s$, and $v \in M(S)$,

$$r'(s,t,c) + \beta \int_{S'} h_v(s',t')\, dq'(s',t' \mid s,t,c)$$

$$= u(c) + \beta v[F(s) - c]$$

$$= r(s,c) + \beta \int_S v(s')\, dq(s' \mid s,c).$$

This completes the proof that (Q') is generated from (Q). Consequently, by Theorem 2.4, if $\pi^*(s)$ solves (Q),

$$\pi^{*\prime}(s,t) = \pi^*(s)$$

solves (Q') and if v^* is the optimal value of (Q), then

$$v^{*\prime}(s,t) = v^*(s)$$

is the optimal value of (Q'). Note that this implies that an optimal policy for (Q') exists that is not time dependent (assuming, as will be shown next, that an optimal policy for (Q) exists). In view of this discussion we can concentrate on solving (Q) in order to obtain a solution of the original problem (P).

Now, for problem (Q), $q(s' \mid s,c)$ is degenerate on $\xi(s,c) = F(s) - c$ and since f is continuous, Corollary 2.2 implies that (2.3) is satisfied (the topology on S and A is the relative topology on S and A obtained from the uusual topology on $\mathbf{R}$). Moreover, r is continuous on $S \times A$ since u is continuous on A. Also, by Theorem 1.2, $D(s)$ is a continuous correspondence on S. Thus, by Corollary 2.1, problem (2.2) of Theorem 2.3 has a solution. Let $g(k)$ be a solution of (2.2). Then by Theorem 2.3, g is an optimal policy and $I(g) = v^*$, where v^* is the unique solution to the optimality equation (v^* exists by Theorem 2.2):

$$v^*(k) = \max_{F(k) \geqslant c \geqslant 0} u(c) + \beta v^*[F(k) - c]. \tag{2.11}$$

We wish to show that the solution of the maximization problem in (2.11) is unique and defines a continuous policy function $g(k)$. First we need

Lemma 2.8 Under Assumption 2.1, v^* is continuous, strictly increasing, and strictly concave. *Bellman's Equation (handwritten)*

Proof Problem (Q) satisfies the assumptions of Corollary 2.1. Thus the operator U previously defined maps bounded, continuous functions into bounded continuous functions, so that v^* is continuous. Using Assumption 2.1, it can be shown that U maps increasing, concave functions into strictly increasing, strictly concave functions (see Exercise 2.10). But if v is any continuous, increasing, concave function, the sequence $U^n v$ for $n = 1, 2, \ldots$ is a sequence of increasing, concave functions that converges uniformly (i.e., in the sup-norm) to v^*. Therefore v^* is increasing and concave. But $v^* = Uv^*$ so v^* is strictly increasing and strictly concave.

Q.E.D.

↓ not strictly preserved by limits (handwritten)

We may now prove

Lemma 2.9 Under Assumption 2.1, problem (Q) has a unique, continuous optimal policy, $g : S \to A$.

Proof Since u, v^*, and f are continuous and strictly concave and $[0, F(k)]$ is compact and convex, the maximization problem defined in (2.11) has a unique solution. By Corollary 2.1, g is continuous. Q.E.D.

Let $h(k) = F(k) - g(k)$, that is, $h(k)$ is next period's capital stock along the optimal path if this period's stock is k. Note that h is continuous since g and F are.

Theorem 2.5 The function v^* is differentiable on $K^0 = (0, B)$, $v^{*\prime} > 0$, $v^{*\prime}$ is strictly decreasing, and, for $k \in K^0$,

$$v^{*\prime}(k) = \beta^{n(k)-1} u'[Q^{n(k)}(k)][dF^{n(k)+1}(k)/dk],$$

where, for any t,

$$Q^t(k) = \text{optimal consumption in period } t \text{ starting from } k_1 = k,$$
$$F^t(k) = \text{composition of } F \text{ with itself } t-1 \text{ times } (F^1(k) \equiv k), \text{ and}$$
$$n(k) = \text{smallest } t \text{ such that } Q^t(k) > 0.$$

If $g(k) > 0$, then $n(k) = 1$ and

$$v^{*\prime}(k) = u'[g(k)]F'(k).$$

limits + U - preserves. (handwritten)

Proof Let $k^0 \in K^0$. We wish to show v^* is differentiable at k^0 by using Lemma 1.4. First suppose $g(k^0) > 0$. Let

$$\pi(k) = \max\{F(k) - h(k^0), 0\} \quad \text{for} \quad k \in [0, B].$$

It is easy to check that π is a feasible policy. Let $v = T_\pi v^*$. Therefore, $v \leq v^*$. But

$$F(k^0) - h(k^0) = g(k^0) > 0,$$

so $\pi(k^0) = g(k^0)$. Therefore, $v(k^0) = v^*(k^0)$.

Now since $\pi(k^0) > 0$ and f is continuous, there is a neighborhood V of k^0 such that $F(k) - h(k^0) > 0$ for every $k \in V$. Thus for $k \in V$, $v(k) = u[F(k) - h(k^0)] + \beta v^*[h(k^0)]$, so that v is differentiable at k and concave (since u and f are). Hence by Lemmas 2.8 and 1.4, v^* is differentiable on V and

$$v^{*\prime}(k) = v'(k) = u'[F(k) - h(k)]F'(k) = u'[g(k)]F'(k).$$

We must now extend the proof to the case in which $g(k^0) = 0$. First define $h^t(k)$ as the composition of h with itself t times for $t = 0, 1, 2, \ldots$ (where $h^0 = i$, the identity map on K). Thus $h^t(k)$ is the optimal capital stock in period $t + 1$ starting from an initial stock of k in period 1. Also define $Q^t(k) = g[h^{t-1}(k)]$ so that $Q^t(k)$ is the optimal consumption in period t if we start with k units of capital in period 1. With $k^0 > 0$, we claim that $Q^t(k^0) > 0$ for some $t \geq 1$, for suppose not, that is,

$$v^*(k^0) = I(g)(k^0) = [1/(1 - \beta)]u(0).$$

Consider the policy $\pi(k) = F(k)$. Then

$$(T_\pi v^*)(k^0) = u(F(k^0)) + \frac{\beta}{1 - \beta} u(0) > \frac{1}{1 - \beta} u(0) = v^*(k^0)$$

since u is strictly increasing and $k^0 > 0$. This contradicts the optimality of g. Thus the assumption that $Q^t(k^0) = 0$ for all t must be false and $Q^t(k^0) > 0$ for some (finite) t.

Let n be the smallest t such that $Q^t(k^0) > 0$. Since we are assuming that $g(k^0) = 0$, $n > 1$. Now let $F^n(k)$ denote the capital stock at date n if $k_1 = k$ and $c_t = 0$ for $t < n$, that is, $F^1(k) = k$, and for $j > 1$,

$$F^j(k) = F[F^{j-1}(k)].$$

Since f is differentiable, F^n is differentiable.

Next define the policy

$$\pi(k) = \max\{F(k) - h^n(k^0), 0\}$$

and let

$$v(k) = \sum_{t=1}^{n-1} \beta^{t-1} u(0) + \beta^{n-1}(T_\pi v^*)(F^n(k))$$

$$= \sum_{t=1}^{n-1} \beta^{t-1} u(0) + \beta^{n-1} u[\pi(F^n(k))] + \beta^n v^*[F^{n+1}(k) - \pi(F^n(k))].$$

Thus $v(k)$ is the value of the plan in which $c_t = 0$ for $t = 1, \ldots, n-1$ (for any k), then $c_n = \pi[F^n(k)]$, and starting at $t = n+1$ the optimal plan is followed. Consequently, $v \leq v^*$. Since $F^n(k^0) = h^{n-1}(k^0)$, $\pi[F^n(k^0)] = Q^n(k^0)$ and so $v(k^0) = v^*(k^0)$. It remains only to show that v is concave in a neighborhood of k^0 and differentiable at k^0, then apply Lemma 1.4. Now

$$F^{n+1}(k^0) - h^n(k^0) > 0,$$

as previously discussed, since $F^n(k^0) = h^{n-1}(k^0)$. Therefore, there is a neighborhood of $F^n(k^0)$, say V_n, such that

$$F(k_n) - h^n(k^0) > 0$$

for all $k_n \in V_n$. But F^n is continuous, being a conposition of continuous functions, so there is a neighborhood, V, of k^0 such that for all $k \in V$, $F^n(k) \in V_n$. Hence for any $k \in V$, $F^{n+1}(k) - h^n(k^0) > 0$, or, for all $k \in V$, $\pi[F^n(k)] = F^{n+1}(k) - h^n(k^0)$. Therefore, for $k \in V$,

$$v(k) = \sum_{t=1}^{n-1} \beta^{t-1} u(0) + \beta^{n-1} u[F^{n+1}(k) - h^n(k^0)] + \beta^n v^*[h^n(k^0)].$$

Since F^n is concave (being a composition of increasing, concave functions), as is u, v is concave for $k \in V$. Also, from the preceding formula, it is clear that v is differentiable for $k \in V$ (and, in particular at k^0), since F^n and u are differentiable. Thus by Lemma 1.4, v^* is differentiable at k^0. Moreover,

$$v^{*\prime}(k^0) = v'(k^0) = \beta^{n-1} u'[Q^n(k^0)][dF^{n+1}(k^0)/dk].$$

The facts that $v^{*\prime} > 0$ and decreasing follow from Lemma 2.8.   Q.E.D.

We may now characterize g by examining the first-order conditions for a solution of the maximization problem in the optimality equation. This condition is

$$u'(c) = \beta v^{*\prime}[F(k) - c] \tag{2.12}$$

for an interior solution $0 < c < F(k)$. In order for $c = 0$ to solve the problem, we must have

$$u'(0) \leq \beta v^{*\prime}[F(k)]. \tag{2.13}$$

Note that, if $u'(0) = \infty$, then $g(k) > 0$ for all $k > 0$. In order for $c = F(k)$ to solve the problem we must have

$$u'[F(k)] \geq \beta v^{*\prime}(0). \tag{2.14}$$

These three cases are depicted graphically in Figure 2.2, panels (a), (b), and (c), respectively. The graphs make use of Theorem 2.5.

Since u' is strictly decreasing and $v^{*\prime}$ is increasing in c but decreasing in k, we see that g is increasing although not strictly. It can also be shown that h is nondecreasing (see Exercise 2.11). We summarize these results in

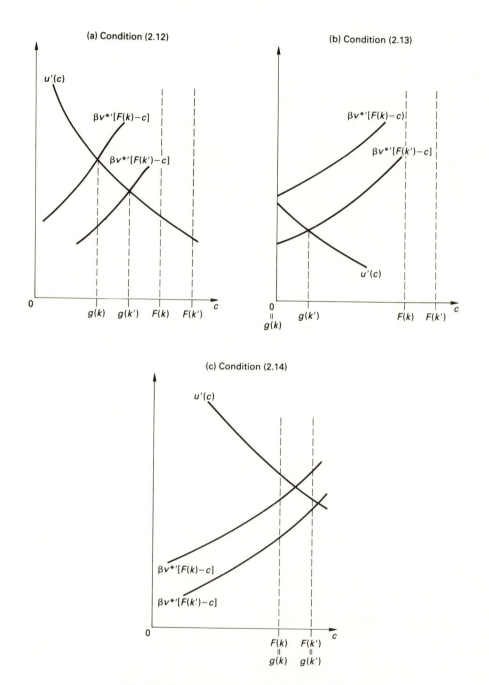

Fig. 2.2 Determination of optimal consumption.

Lemma 2.10 If g solves (P) and h is defined as just discussed, then g is monotone increasing on K and h is monotone increasing on K. Consequently, $\{k_t^*\}$ (defined by $k_t^* = h(k_{t-1}^*)$ for $t > 1$, $k_1^* = \bar{k}$) is either a monotone increasing or decreasing sequence.

We now wish to show that, along the optimal path, k_t either increases or decreases to a rest point (or steady-state) capital k^* and characterize this point.

Theorem 2.6 If $f'(0) > \rho + \delta$ [or, $F'(0) > 1 + \rho$], where $\rho = (1/\beta) - 1$ [or $\beta = 1/(1 + \rho)$], then the unique value k^* satisfying $f'(k^*) = \rho + \delta$ (see Figure 2.3) is the unique fixed point of $h(k)$ on $(0, B)$. Moreover, for any $k > k^*$, $h(k) < k$ and for any $k < k^*$, $h(k) > k$. Consequently, if $0 < \bar{k} < k^*$, then k_t^* is strictly monotone increasing and $k_t^* \to k^*$. Similarly, if $\bar{k} > k^*$, then k_t^* is strictly monotone decreasing and $k_t^* \to k^*$. If $\bar{k} = k^*$, then $k_t^* = k^*$ for every t. Thus k^* is the unique steady-state capital to which the optimal path of capital converges. (turnpike)

Proof First, to establish that k^* exists, we have by assumption that $f'(0) > \rho + \delta$ and $f'(k_m) = \delta < \rho + \delta$ (see Figure 2.3). Therefore, since f' is continuous, there is $k^* \in (0, k_m)$ such that $f'(k^*) = \rho + \delta$. Moreover, by strict concavity of f, k^* is unique.

Next we must show that k^* is the unique fixed point of $h(k)$, that is, $h(k^*) = k^*$. First, we claim that $h(k) < k$ for all $k \geq \hat{k}$. Suppose $k > \hat{k}$. Then $h(k) = F(k) - g(k) < k$ since $k > \hat{k}$ and $g(k) \geq 0$. If $k = \hat{k}$, then clearly $h(\hat{k}) \leq \hat{k}$. But $h(\hat{k}) \neq \hat{k}$ since if $k_1 = \hat{k}$, the policy g would involve zero consumption in every period, and we know that, with $k_1 > 0$, that policy can be dominated.

Now we wish to show that if $0 < k < k^*$, then $h(k) > k$. Note that by the strict concavity of f, if $k < k^*$, then $F'(k) > 1/\beta$ (see Figure 2.3). First, if $g(k) = 0$, then $h(k) = F(k) > k$ since $0 < k < k^* < \hat{k}$, and we are done. So suppose $g(k) > 0$. Now assume $h(k) \leq k$ and derive a contradiction. Since $v^{*\prime}$ is decreasing and we are assuming $h(k) \leq k$,

$$\beta v^{*\prime}[h(k)] \geq \beta v^{*\prime}(k)$$
$$= \beta u'[g(k)]F'(k) \quad \text{by Theorem 2.5 since } g(k) > 0$$
$$> u'[g(k)] \quad \text{since } F'(k) > 1/\beta.$$

But $g(k) > 0$ so $g(k)$ must satisfy either (2.12) or (2.14). Either condition contradicts the above inequality.

Since h is continuous and $h(k) > k$ for $0 < k < k^*$ and $h(k) < k$ for $k \geq \hat{k}$, there must be at least one $k \in [k^*, \hat{k})$ such that $h(k) = k$. Let k be any such fixed point of h. Then $g(k) = F(k) - h(k) = f(k) - \delta k > 0$ since $h(k) = k$ and $k < \hat{k}$. Also $g(k) < F(k)$ since $h(k) = k > 0$. Therefore, $g(k)$ must satisfy the first-order condition (2.12), that is,

$$u'[g(k)] = \beta v^{*\prime}[h(k)]$$
$$= \beta v^{*\prime}(k) \quad \text{since } h(k) = k$$
$$= \beta u'[g(k)]F'(k) \quad \text{by Theorem 2.5 since } g(k) > 0,$$

or

$$F'(k) = 1/\beta \quad \text{since } u' > 0.$$

Therefore, k must be the unique point k^*. We have thus far shown that h has a unique fixed point k^* in $(0, \hat{k})$ and k^* satisfies $f'(k^*) = \rho + \delta$.

We must now show that if $k > k^*$, $h(k) < k^*$. We have already shown this for $k \geq \hat{k}$ so suppose $k \in (k^*, \hat{k})$. If $h(k) \geq k$, then since $h(\hat{k}) < \hat{k}$ and h is continuous, there is a $k' \in (k, \hat{k})$ such that $h(k') = k'$. But $k' \geq k > k^*$, which contradicts the result that k^* is the unique fixed point of h.

To prove the last part, note that if $\bar{k} = k^*$, then $h(\bar{k}) = k^*$ so $k_t^* = k^*$ for all t. If $0 < \bar{k} < k^*$, since $h(k) > k$ for $0 < k < k^*$, $\{k_t^*\}$ is a strictly monotone increasing sequence. Since $k_t^* \in K$ for each t and K is compact, k_t^* must converge to a unique point, say k^0. But $h(k_t^*) = k_{t+1}^*$ and h is

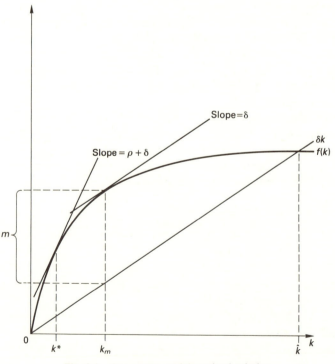

Fig. 2.3 One-sector model, optimal solution.

continuous so

$$\lim_{t \to \infty} h(k_t^*) = \lim_{t \to \infty} k_{t+1}^* \quad \text{or} \quad h(k^0) = k^0.$$

Thus $k^0 = k^*$. The proof for $\bar{k} > k^*$ is exactly analogous.   Q.E.D.

To summarize, we have so far characterized an optimal solution to the one-sector growth model, namely,

$$c_t^* = g(k_t^*),$$

$$k_{t+1}^* = h(k_t^*) \quad \text{for every } t = 1, 2, \ldots,$$

and

$$k_1^* = \bar{k}.$$

Moreover, $k_t^* \uparrow k^*$ if $\bar{k} < k^*$ and $k_t^* \downarrow k^*$ if $\bar{k} > k^*$, where k^* satisfies $f'(k^*) = \rho + \delta$. The behavior of c_t^* is derived from $c_t^* = F(k_t^*) - k_{t+1}^*$ and the behavior of k_t^*. Note that the steady-state capital stock k^* is associated with a steady state consumption $c^* = f(k^*) - \delta k^*$. The fact that the optimal capital stock converges to a steady state is often referred to as a "Turnpike Theorem."

It remains to show the existence of a competitive equilibrium. This involves showing the existence of a valuation equilibrium and then deriving the corresponding prices. This is done in Chapter 3.

EXERCISES

2.1. Prove Lemma 2.2.

2.2. Verify that if c is any constant, then for any π, and any $u \in M(S)$, $T_\pi(u + c) = T_\pi u + \beta c$.

2.3. Prove Corollary 2.2.

2.4. Prove Lemma 2.7.

2.5. Show that $S' = \bigcup_{s \in S} E_s$ and that the sets E_s are nonempty and pairwise disjoint, where S' and E_s are defined following Lemma 2.7.

2.6. *Formulate* (you needn't solve) the following problem as a dynamic programming problem, that is, define the state space, S, the action space, A, the action choice correspondence, D, the equation of motion, q, the return function r, and write the optimality equation:

You are told that an unknown number has been drawn from a uniform distribution on the integers $1, 2, \ldots, N$. You wish to minimize the expected number of tries to guess the number. On each try, you propose a number and are told (truthfully) whether the unknown number is above, below, or equal to the proposed number.

2.7. Suppose

$$u(c) = \ell nc$$

$$F(k) = \gamma k^\alpha \quad \text{for some } \gamma > 0,\ 0 < \alpha < 1.$$

Compute $\hat{k}$ and k_m for this problem. Show that the optimality equation has a solution of the form

$$u^*(k) = a + b\ell nk$$

and find the correct values of a and b. Next derive the unique solution of problem (2.2) of Theorem 2.3. Note that even though u is not continuous or bounded on A and the optimal value function is not continuous or bounded on S, the solution of problem (2.2) is still an optimal solution of (Q) for this case. Also find the function $h(k)$ that gives the optimal value of next period's state given the current state, k. Finally compute the unique steady-state value of k (i.e., a k^* such that if $k_t = k^*$, then $k_{t+1} = k^*$ along the optimal path). Show that the steady-state is stable, that is, that $k_t \to k^*$ along the optimal path.

2.8. A monopolist has the following production technology. Given current capacity, Q, he can produce any amount of output, q, up to Q units at zero cost, but he cannot produce more than Q in the current period. Capacity can be increased over time but cannot be sold. Any nonnegative amount a of capacity can be added in any period at cost $c(a) = a^2$, but the new capacity cannot be used until the next period. The monopolist faces the same demand for his product each period given by $q = 1 - p$, where p is the price of output. Answer the following questions:

(1) What does the assumption about demand imply about how consumers take account of the future in this model?
(2) Formulate the monopolist's problem as a stationary, discounted, dynamic programming problem assuming that he seeks to maximize the present value over an infinite horizon of the flow of profits. Assume his discount factor is $0 < \beta < 1$. (Remember what formulate means from Exercise 2.6.)
(3) Show that the solution is given by

$$u^*(Q) = \begin{cases} \alpha & \text{for } Q \geq \tfrac{1}{2} \\ \delta + \gamma Q(1 - Q) & \text{for } Q \leq \tfrac{1}{2}, \end{cases}$$

where α and δ are constants and

$$\gamma = \frac{2\beta - 1 + [1 + 4\beta^2]^{1/2}}{2\beta},$$

and that the optimal policy is

$$a^* = g(Q) = \begin{cases} 0 & \text{for } Q \geq \frac{1}{2}, \\ \beta\gamma(\frac{1}{2} - Q)/(1 + \beta\gamma) & \text{for } Q \leq \frac{1}{2}. \end{cases}$$

Determine α.

2.9. Suppose you own a share of stock in Dounenout Corporation. In addition, you own an open-ended *put option* on this share, that is, you have the right to sell the share at any time for an "exercise price" of X. The stock pays a dividend $\tilde{d}_t$ in period t, $t = 1, 2, \ldots$, where $\{\tilde{d}_t\}$ is a Markov process with transition function $F(d', d) = \Pr[\tilde{d}_{t+1} \leq d' \mid \tilde{d}_t = d]$. Assume that the stock market is efficient so that you are always indifferent between selling the share in the market and keeping it (in this case, it doesn't matter whether you actually own the stock currently or simply can buy it at the market price). Finally suppose you are risk neutral, and you discount future payments using the discount factor β.

(1) Formulate the problem of choosing an optimal exercise date as a stationary, discounted, dynamic programming problem. (*Hint*: Assume the choice variable $a_t = 0$ if you don't exercise at t, $a_t = 1$ if you do. Also, one of the state variables must indicate whether the put has been exercised, since once it has been exercised, it cannot be exercised again. Finally, in defining the return function r, use the flow equivalent of the exercise price, that is, a once and for all payment of X is equivalent to a periodic payment, starting immediately, of $x = X(1 - \beta)$ forever.) Assume that if you exercise at t, you receive X but not the current dividend d_t.

(2) For the remainder of the problem, assume that F is monotone decreasing in d for all d', that is, if today's dividend increases, then tomorrow's dividend increases in the first order stochastic dominance sense. Show that the optimal value function u^* is increasing in the current dividend, d.

(3) Show that the optimal policy involves a reservation value of d, say d^*, such that exercise is optimal if and only if $d \leq d^*$.

(4) Show that if $\{\tilde{d}_t\}$ is i.i.d., that is, F is independent of d, then d^* satisfies

$$X = d^* + [\beta/(1 - \beta p^*)][X(1 - p^*) + \bar{d}(d^*)p^*],$$

where $p^* = 1 - F(d^*)$ and $\bar{d}(d^*) = E[\tilde{d} \mid \tilde{d} \geq d^*]$, or

$$x = d^*(1 - \beta p^*) + \bar{d}(d^*)\beta p^*,$$

where $x = X(1 - \beta)$ is the flow equivalent of the exercise price.

(5) Assuming $\{\bar{d}_t\}$ is i.i.d. and $\bar{d}_t$ is uniform on $[0, 1]$, show that

$$d^* = \begin{cases} \dfrac{1}{\beta}[-(1-\beta) + \sqrt{1 - 2\beta(1-x)}] & \text{for } x > \beta/2, \\ 0 & \text{for } x \leq \beta/2. \end{cases}$$

Note that, for $x \leq \beta/2$, one never exercises the put. Also $d^* < x$ (except at $x = 1$, where $d^* = 1$), so that one does not exercise the put even though the current dividend on the stock is less than the flow value of exercising the put, and the current dividend provides no information about future dividends in this case. The reason is that it is worth $x - d^*$ to keep the option open to exercise later if d is smaller than d^*.

(6) Assume $\{\bar{d}_t\}$ is a Markov chain on $\{0, 1, 2\}$, that is, F can be represented by the transition matrix (π_{ij}), $i = 0, 1, 2$, $j = 0, 1, 2$, where $\pi_{ij} = \Pr(d' = i \mid d = j)$. Construct a spreadsheet using a popular software package such as 1-2-3[4] to calculate the optimal policy.

2.10. Using Assumption 2.1, show that the operator U, defined after Lemma 2.4, as applied to the one-sector growth model, maps increasing, concave functions into strictly increasing, strictly concave functions.

2.11. Show that h (the optimal capital for next period as a function of this period's capital) is also nondecreasing. (*Hint*: This can be shown using the graphs of Figure 2.2 by showing that the $v^{*\prime}$ curve shifts rightward by the amount $\Delta[F(k)]$ when there is an increase in k and using the fact that u' is strictly decreasing in c.)

2.12. Prove that if $\bar{k} < k^*$, then $c_t^* \uparrow c^*$ if $\bar{k} > k^*$, $c_t^* \downarrow c^*$.

NOTES

1. The model is called a one-sector model because the assumed technology of producing consumption and capital goods is that they are perfect substitutes. That is, net output in any period t, $F(k_t)$, can be divided in any way between consumption in that period, c_t, and capital for next period, k_{t+1}; in other words, the transformation curve between consumption goods and capital is a straight line of slope -1. The origins of the model can be traced back to Ramsey (1928) who considered a model of optimal growth without discounting. The formulation of the one-sector production technology used here is due to Solow (1956). Solow, however, did not consider optimal growth (he assumed a constant saving rate). The first analysis of this model in an optimizing framework was in independent work by Cass (1965a, 1965b) and Koopmans (1963).

2. Most of the development that follows is based on Blackwell (1965) and Denardo (1967).

3. The norm defined here is almost the same as the essential supremum norm defined in Chapter 1 for the space L_∞. The difference is that this norm is affected by the behavior of the function on sets of zero measure.
4. 1–2–3 is a trademark of Lotus Development Corporation.
5. Some familiarity with how spreadsheet programs work is assumed.

REFERENCES

Blackwell, D., "Discounted Dynamic Programming," *Annals of Mathematical Statistics,* **36** (1965), pp. 226–235.

Cass, D., "Optimal Growth in an Aggregate Model of Capital Accumulation," *Review of Economic Studies,* **32,** 3 (July 1965, 1965a), pp. 233–240.

————— *Studies in the Theory of Optimal Growth,* unpublished Ph.D. dissertation, Stanford University, 1965 (1965b).

Denardo, E. V., "Contraction Mappings in the Theory Underlying Dynamic Programming," *SIAM Review,* **9,** 2 (April 1967), pp. 165–177.

Kolmogorov, A. N. and S. V. Fomin, *Introductory Real Analysis* (New York: Dover, 1970),

Koopmans, T. C., "On the Concept of Optimal Economic Growth," Cowles Foundation Discussion Paper No. 163, Cowles Foundation for Research in Economics at Yale University, 1963.

Ramsey, F. P., "A Mathematical Theory of Saving," *Economic Journal* (Sept. 1928), pp. 543–559.

Solow, R. M., "A Contribution to the Theory of Economic Growth," *Quarterly Journal of Economics* (Feb. 1956), pp. 65–94.

CHAPTER 3

Valuation Equilibrium and Pareto Optimality

It has been established in the case of a finite-dimensional commodity space, that (1) every competitive equilibrium is a Pareto optimum and (2) every Pareto optimum can be supported as a competitive equilibrium. It is the task of this chapter to present a concept of competitive equilibrium for models with infinite-dimensional commodity spaces and examine the relationship between competitive equilibrium and Pareto optimality in this case.[1] As mentioned in Chapter 1, we are interested in such models because they can be used to represent economies with infinitely lived agents or with an infinite number of possible states of the world (or both). The equivalence between Pareto optimality and competitive equilibrium can be used to characterize a competitive equilibrium by solving for a Pareto optimal allocation.

First we introduce the equilibrium concept considered in this chapter, namely, valuation equilibrium [Debreu (1954)]. The concept is called valuation equilibrium because the equilibrium is characterized by a linear valuation functional that assigns a value to each commodity bundle. In general, this valuation functional may not be representable as prices. That is, with infinite-dimensional commodity spaces, there may be no price vector such that the value of a commodity bundle is the inner product of the price vector and the quantity vector. This may be the case even though the valuation functional is linear (recall from Chapter 1 that with finite-dimensional spaces, a linear function can always be represented as an inner product). Consequently, in the second section of this chapter, some sufficient conditions are given for the valuation equilibrium to have a price representation. Finally, in the third section, we apply the new tools developed in the first two sections to the one-sector model familiar from Chapter 2.

3.1 VALUATION EQUILIBRIUM

In a valuation equilibrium, all trading takes place at date 1. The commodities traded are promises to deliver certain goods at specified dates contingent on specified events in return for certain goods delivered at date 1. Such arrangements may be called "commodity bond contracts" because they involve a current payment in return for a promise to deliver a contingent future payment. Markets are assumed to be complete in the sense that for each good, date, and event that can be distinguished at that date, there is a market for promises to deliver that good on that date contingent on that event. Note that this implies that information is symmetrically distributed across economic agents. If one agent can distinguish a certain event at some given date, then so can all agents. Otherwise contracts to deliver contingent on that event would not be enforceable.

We begin with some notation. Let L be a real normed vector space of commodity points (L can be a space of infinite sequences or of continuous functions). The ith consumer ($i = 1, \ldots, m$) has a consumption set $X_i \subset L$ that contains every (technologically) feasible consumption point. If, for example, it includes labor supply $\{n_t\}$, then the condition $0 \leqslant n_t \leqslant 1$, $t = 1, 2, \ldots$ may be one of the constraints defining X_i (note that the budget constraint is not a technological constraint and hence does not restrict X_i). As a sign convention, components of $x_i \in X_i$ that are outputs (i.e., purchased by consumers) are assumed to be nonnegative; components that are inputs (purchased by firms) are nonpositive. Preferences of a consumer are described by a complete preordering $\geqslant_i$ on L (or at least on X_i).[2] If x_i is at least as desired as x_i', then

$$x_i \geqslant_i x_i'.$$

If both

$$x_i \geqslant_i x_i' \quad \text{and} \quad x_i' \geqslant_i x_i, \quad \text{then} \quad x_i \sim_i x_i'.$$

If

$$x_i \geqslant_i x_i' \quad \text{but not} \quad x_i' \geqslant_i x_i, \quad \text{then} \quad x_i >_i x_i'.$$

Finally, $x_i^S \in X_i$ is a saturation point for i if

$$x_i^S \geqslant_i x_i \quad \text{for every } x_i \in X_i.$$

There are n producers, and the jth producer ($j = 1, \ldots, n$) has a production set $Y_j \subset L$ that contains all technologically feasible combinations of outputs (positive) and inputs (negative). Let

$$x \equiv \sum_{i=1}^{m} x_i \quad \text{and} \quad y \equiv \sum_{j=1}^{n} y_j$$

denote total consumption and total production, respectively. An alloca-
tion, $[(x_i), (y_j)]$ is said to be *attainable* if $x - y = \zeta$, where $\zeta \in L$ denotes
exogenously determined resources available.

As an example of the type of economy being modeled, suppose each of
m consumers has one unit of time per period that can either be consumed
or supplied to firms. Further suppose that there are n firms each producing
the same perishable physical consumption good, called "shmoos," using
only labor input.[3] In particular, there is no capital good and no
uncertainty. The commodity space for this example is given by the set of
infinite sequences of consumption of shmoos and supply of labor over
time, that is,

$$L = \{\{x_t\} = \{x_{1t}, x_{2t})\} \mid \|\{x_{it}\}\|_\infty < \infty, \ i = 1, 2\}$$

where x_{1t} is interpreted as consumption of shmoos at date t and x_{2t} is
interpreted as supply of labor at date t. Note that x_{2t} is assumed to be
nonpositive since it is purchased by firms. Also note that the commodity
space must have a norm. We have chosen the sup norm and assumed that
consumption and labor supply are bounded in this norm. This is a typical
assumption for economies without uncertainty. The consumption set for
consumer i is given by

$$X_i = \{x \in L \mid x_{1t} \geq 0, \ 0 \geq x_{2t} \geq -1, \ t = 1, 2, \ldots\}.$$

The constraint that $x_{2t} \geq -1$ reflects the assumption that each consumer
has at most one unit of time per period. Consumer preferences may be
represented by a utility function such as

$$U_i(x) = \sum_{t=1}^{\infty} \beta_i^t u_i(x_{1t}, x_{2t}) \quad \text{for } x \in X_i,$$

where β_i is a "discount factor" for i, and u_i is a period utility function for i
that is increasing in both arguments (since labor supply is measured in the
negative direction, an increase in x_{2t} reflects a decrease in labor supplied in
period t).[4]

The production possibilities for this economy could be represented by
firm-specific production functions $f_j : \mathbf{R}_- \to \mathbf{R}$, that is, the production
possibility set of firm j is given by

$$Y_j = \{y \in L \mid 0 \leq y_{1t} \leq f_j(y_{2t}), \ y_{2t} \leq 0, \ t = 1, 2, \ldots\}.$$

This production possibility set is represented in Figure 3.1. Note that,
because labor supply is measured in the negative direction, f_j is downward
sloping. Also note that, in this example, the production possibilities in one
period do not depend on inputs in any other period. This would not be the
case if, for example, firms were to invest in durable capital goods.

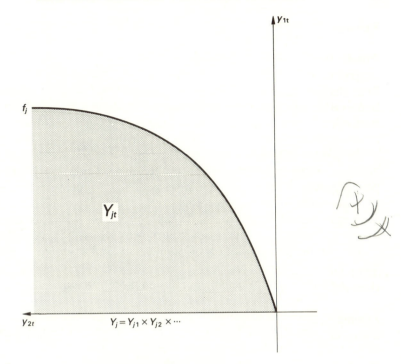

Fig. 3.1 Production possibility sets.

There are no exogeneous resources available in this economy, so ζ is the zero vector in L. Therefore, an allocation $[(x_i),(y_j)]$ is attainable if

$$\sum_{i=1}^{m} x_{i1t} - \sum_{j=1}^{n} y_{j1t} = 0 \quad \text{for all } t$$

and

$$\sum_{i=1}^{m} x_{i2t} - \sum_{j=1}^{n} y_{j2t} = 0 \quad \text{for all } t.$$

If we assume that there are prices

$$p = \{(p_{1t}, p_{2t})\}$$

giving the amount of the consumption good one must pay at $t = 1$ in return for delivery of either consumption good (p_{1t}) or labor (p_{2t}) at date t, then we may write the budget constraint of the ith consumer and the profit function of the jth firm as

$$px_i = \sum_{t=1}^{\infty} (p_{1t}x_{i1t} + p_{2t}x_{i2t}) \leq 0$$

and

$$py_j = \sum_{t=1}^{\infty} (p_{1t}y_{j1t} + p_{2t}y_{j2t}).$$

Note that, since labor supply is measured in the negative direction, the terms in the consumer's budget constraint involving x_{i2t} represent income for the consumer, and the terms in the firm's profit function involving y_{j2t} represent costs for the firm. Also note that, because of the interpretation of the commodities and prices, the expenditure expression on the left side of the budget constraint and the profit function must be interpreted as present values. That is, p_{1t} is the price paid now for delivery of one shmoo at date t while p_{2t} is the price paid now for delivery of one unit of labor services at date t. These prices do not correspond to the usual price for consumption goods and the wage, respectively. Note, however, that p_{1t}/p_{2t} is the current *forward* price of shmoos in terms of labor for date t delivery.[5]

We are now ready to define equilibrium more formally.

Definition 3.1 A *valuation equilibrium* is an attainable allocation $[(x_i^0), (y_j^0)]$ and a linear form (i.e., a linear functional that is continuous with respect to the norm topology) v on L such that

$$\text{for every } i, \text{ if } x_i \in X_i, \ v(x_i) \leq v(x_i^0), \text{ then } x_i \leq_i x_i^0, \qquad (3.1)$$

$$\text{for every } j, \text{ if } y_j \in Y_j, \text{ then } v(y_j) \leq v(y_j^0). \qquad (3.2)$$

We may interpret v as cost or value of a commodity point. Then (3.1) guarantees that at an equilibrium, each consumer will be maximizing his satisfaction under a budget constraint and (3.2) guarantees that each firm will be maximizing profits (or net value of output). An arbitrary linear form v is introduced since it may not always be possible to find a sequence of prices for L (such as was assumed in the example above). Conditions under which this may be done are given in the next section.

We want to establish the two fundamental theorems of welfare economics with respect to a valuation equilibrium. First, we define Pareto optimality.

Definition 3.2 $[(x_i^0), (y_i^0)]$ is a *Pareto optimum* if it is attainable and there is no attainable allocation $[(x_i), (y_j)]$ such that $x_i \geq_i x_i^0$ for every i and $x_i >_i x_i^0$ for at least one i. Some

The first theorem, showing a valuation equilibrium to be a Pareto optimum, requires two assumptions.

Assumption 3.1 For every i, X_i is convex (convexity of the consumption set).

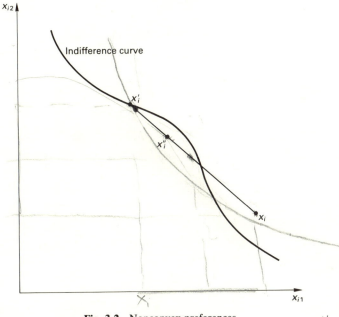

Fig. 3.2 Nonconvex preferences.

Assumption 3.2 If $x_i, x_i' \in X_i$ and $x_i' <_i x_i$, then $x_i' <_i (1-t)x_i' + tx_i$ for every $t \in (0,1)$, for every i (convexity of preferences).

Assumption 3.2 rules out indifference curves like the one shown in Figure 3.2. In the figure, x_i'' is a convex combination of x_i and x_i' and $x_i >_i x_i'$, but $x_i' >_i x_i''$.

Theorem 3.1 Under Assumptions 3.1 and 3.2, if $[(x_i^0), (y_j^0), v]$ is a valuation equilibrium and for every i, x_i^0 is not a saturation point, then $[(x_i^0), (y_j^0)]$ is a Pareto optimum.

Proof [Debreu (1954, p. 589)]. From the definition of valuation equilibrium, if $x_i \in X_i$ and $x_i >_i x_i^0$, then x_i must be more expensive than x_i^0, that is, $v(x_i) > v(x_i^0)$. Now suppose that $x_i \in X_i$ and $x_i \sim_i x_i^0$. Since x_i^0 is not a saturation point, we can choose $x_i' \in X_i$ such that $x_i' >_i x_i^0$. Therefore, $x_i' >_i x_i$. Consider $x_i(t) = (1-t)x_i + tx_i'$. By Assumption 3.2, for all $t \in (0,1)$, $x_i(t) >_i x_i$. Consequently, from the foregoing we have

$$v(x_i^0) < v(x_i(t)) = (1-t)v(x_i) + tv(x_i').$$

Taking limits of both sides as t approaches zero gives $v(x_i^0) \leq v(x_i)$.

Now consider an allocation $[(x_i), (y_i)]$ and suppose that each consumer prefers x_i to x_i^0 with strict preference for at least one consumer. From the foregoing, we have

$$\sum_{i=1}^{m} v(x_i) > \sum_{i=1}^{m} v(x_i^0),$$

or, using the linearity of v, $v(x) > v(x^0)$. On the other hand, profit maximization (3.2) implies that $v(y) \le v(y^0)$. Combining these two inequalities gives

$$v(x) - v(y) > v(x^0) - v(y^0)$$

or

$$v(x - y) > v(\zeta),$$

since v is linear and $x^0 - y^0 = \zeta$. This last inequality implies that $x - y \ne \zeta$, that is, the allocation $[(x_i), (y_i)]$ is not attainable.   Q.E.D.

In order to establish Theorem 3.2, we need three more assumptions in addition to Assumptions 3.1 and 3.2. Let

$$I(x_i', x_i'') \equiv \{t \in \mathbf{R} \mid (1 - t)x_i' + tx_i'' \in X_i\}$$

for the points x_i', $x_i'' \in X_i$. Note that $(1 - t)x_i' + tx_i''$ is a *linear* (not convex) combination.

Assumption 3.3   Let $x_i \in X_i$. Then, for every i, x_i', $x_i'' \in X_i$, the sets

$$\{t \in I(x_i', x_i'') \mid (1 - t)x_i' + tx_i'' \succeq_i x_i\}$$

and

$$\{t \in I(x_i', x_i'') \mid (1 - t)x_i' + tx_i'' \preceq_i x_i\}$$

are closed in $I(x_i', x_i'')$ relative to the usual topology on $\mathbf{R}$.

Assumption 3.4 $Y \equiv \sum_{j=1}^{n} Y_j$ is convex.

Assumption 3.5   Either L is finite dimensional, or Y has a nonempty interior.

Some intuition regarding Assumption 3.3 can be obtained by considering the case $X_i = \mathbf{R}_+^2$. In Figure 3.3, the line AD is $I(x_i', x_i'')$, the segment BC is the first set and the two segments AB and CD make up the second set. The assumption is that BC and $AB \cup CD$ are both closed in AD.

The lexicographic ordering provides an example of preferences that do not satisfy Assumption 3.3. A lexicographic ordering on a two-dimensional commodity space is defined as follows: (x_1, x_2) is preferred to (x_1', x_2') if and only if $x_1 > x_1'$ or $x_1 = x_1'$ and $x_2 \ge x_2'$. That such preferences do not satisfy

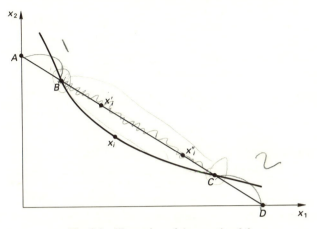

Fig. 3.3 Illustration of Assumption 3.3.

Assumption 3.3 is illustrated in Figure 3.4. In this case the first set is represented by the closed interval $[B,D]$, but the second is represented by the half open interval $[A,B]$.

Assumption 3.4 implies "aggregate" non-increasing returns to scale. Note that it is weaker than the assumption that Y_j is convex for every j. The more relevant part of Assumption 3.5 is, of course, the latter. Interior is defined relative to the norm-topology on L, that is, $y_0 \in \text{Int}(Y)$ if and only if there exists $\varepsilon > 0$ such that $\|y - y_0\| < \varepsilon$ implies $y \in Y$. Note also that the free disposal assumption implies that the interior of Y is nonempty.[6]

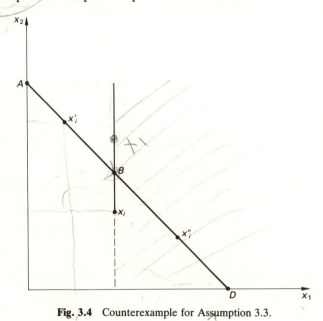

Fig. 3.4 Counterexample for Assumption 3.3.

Theorem 3.2 Under Assumptions 3.1–3.5, with every Pareto optimal allocation $[(x_i^0), (y_j^0)]$ such that x_i^0 is not a saturation point for some i, is associated a non-trivial linear form v on L such that $[(x_i^0), (y_i^0), v]$ is a *quasi-valuation equilibrium*, that is,

$$\text{for every } i, \text{ if } x_i \in X_i \text{ and } x_i \geq_i x_i^0, \text{ then } v(x_i) \geq v(x_i^0), \qquad (3.3)$$

$$\text{for every } j, \text{ if } y_j \in Y_j, \text{ then } v(y_j) \leq v(y_j^0). \qquad (3.4)$$

Proof [Debreu (1954, p. 590)]. Suppose x_i' and x_i'' are in X_i with $x_i' \leq_i x_i''$. By Assumption 3.3, the set $\{t \in I(x_i', x_i'') \mid (1-t)x_i' + tx_i'' <_i x_i'\}$ is open in $I(x_i', x_i'')$. Therefore, its intersection with the open interval $(0,1)$ is open. We wish to show that this intersection is empty. Suppose not. Then it would contain at least two elements, say $t_1 < t_2$. Let x_i^1 and x_i^2 be the corresponding convex combinations of x_i' and x_i''. By choice of t_1, $x_i^1 <_i x_i' \leq_i x_i''$. But, since x_i^2 is a convex combination of x_i' and x_i'', by Assumption 3.2, $x_i^1 <_i x_i^2$. If we replace t_1 and x_i^1 in the previous two sentences by t_2 and x_i^2, these statements are still valid, and we may conclude that $x_i^2 <_i x_i^1$. This contradiction implies that the intersection of the above set with $(0,1)$ is empty. Consequently, for all $t \in [0,1]$,

$$x_i' \leq_i (1-t)x_i' + tx_i'' \in X_i.$$

It follows immediately that the sets $\bar{X}_i(x_i^0)$ consisting of all bundles in X_i that are preferred to x_i^0 and $X_i(x_i^0)$ consisting of all bundles in X_i that are strictly preferred to x_i^0 are convex.

Let i' be a consumer for whom $x_{i'}^0$ is not a saturation point. Consider the set

$$Z = X_{i'}(x_{i'}^0) + \sum_{i \neq i'} \bar{X}_i(x_i^0) - \sum_{j=1}^n Y_j.$$

Suppose $\zeta \in Z$. Then, for some allocation, $[(x_i), (y_i)]$, $\zeta = x - y$, where (x_i) Pareto dominates (x_i^0). This contradicts the assumption that $[(x_i^0), (y_i^0)]$ is a Pareto optimum. Therefore, ζ is not a member of Z. Now Z is convex, being the sum of convex sets, and if Y has an interior point, so does Z. Therefore, the "Support Theorem" [Luenberger (1969, Theorem 2, p. 133)] guarantees that there is a nontrivial linear form v on L such that $v(z) \geq v(\zeta)$ for all $z \in Z$. Since $\zeta = x^0 - y^0$, if $x_{i'} \in X_{i'}(x_{i'}^0)$ and $x_i \in \bar{X}_i(x_i^0)$, for $i \neq i'$, and $y_j \in Y_j$, for all j, we have

$$v\left[\sum_i (x_i - x_i^0) - \sum_j (y_j - y_j^0)\right] \geq 0.$$

In the preceding statement $X_{i'}(x_{i'}^0)$ can be replaced by $\bar{X}_{i'}(x_{i'}^0)$ since any $x_{i'}$ such that $x_{i'} \sim_{i'} x_{i'}^0$ is the limit of points in $X_{i'}(x_{i'}^0)$. Therefore,

$$\sum_i v(x_i - x_i^0) + \sum_j v(y_j^0 - y_j) \geq 0,$$

for all $x_i \in \bar{X}_i(x_i^0)$ and $y_j \in Y_j$. In particular, we can choose (x_i) and (y_j) such that $x_i = x_i^0$ for all but one i and $y_j = y_j^0$ for all j. Then the preceding inequality implies that, for the chosen i, $v(x_i) \geqslant v(x_i^0)$. Obviously this can be done for each i, thus establishing (3.3). A similar argument establishes (3.4).   Q.E.D.

We want v to be non-trivial, since otherwise v takes every point into 0, thus trivially satisfying (3.3) and (3.4). Theorem 3.2 does not quite correspond to the standard second theorem of welfare economics since (3.3) does not necessarily imply (3.1) in the definition of a valuation equilibrium. In other words, we might have a case where an allocation is Pareto optimal but does not maximize satisfaction under the budget constraint for any valuation function (hence not a valuation equilibrium). As an illustration of this case, consider a one-consumer, one-firm economy where X and Y are as in Figure 3.5 ($X = \mathbf{R}_+^2 \cap \{x \mid v(x) \geqslant v(\bar{x})\}$, where v is a linear function of x). x^0 is a Pareto optimum since no other point in $X \cap Y$ (the thick line) can make the consumer better off. Clearly $[(x^0), (x^0), v]$ in the illustration is a quasi-valuation equilibrium. It is not, however, a valuation equilibrium since x^0 does not maximize satisfaction under the budget constraint (x' is preferred to x^0). The following Lemma states the condition under which this case cannot happen.

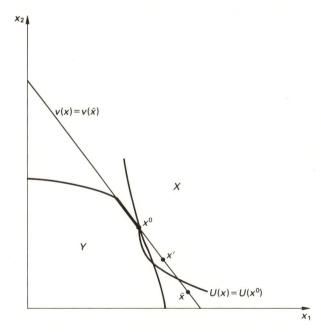

Fig. 3.5 Quasi-valuation versus valuation equilibrium.

Lemma 3.1 Under Assumptions 3.1–3.3, if for every i there is $x_i' \in X_i$ such that $v(x_i') < v(x_i^0)$, then (3.3) implies (3.1).

Proof [Debreu (1954, p. 591)] Choose $x_i \in X_i$ such that $v(x_i) \leq v(x_i^0)$. Let $x_i(t) = (1 - t)x_i + tx_i'$. Then for any $t \in (0,1)$, $v(x_i(t)) < v(x_i^0)$. Consequently, by the contrapositive of (3.3), $x_i(t) <_i x_i^0$ for $0 < t < 1$. By Assumption 3.3, $\{t \in I(x_i, x_i') \mid x_i(t) \leq_i x_i^0\}$ is closed in $I(x_i, x_i')$. Also, we have just seen that this set contains $(0,1)$. Therefore, by continuity, it contains 0, that is, $x_i \leq_i x_i^0$.   Q.E.D.

3.2 PRICE REPRESENTATION OF VALUATION EQUILIBRIA

In the previous section, the desirable correspondence between valuation equilibrium and Pareto optimality is shown to hold under the given assumptions. The valuation function, or pricing scheme, however, may not in general take the more familiar form of an inner product.[7] In this section we develop inner product representations of pricing schemes for two particular cases, one for infinite time horizon and one for uncertainty, following Prescott–Lucas (1972).

The environment is essentially the same as in the previous section, and we still need the first two assumptions that were required for establishing Theorem 3.1. For convenience, we reproduce them here:

Assumption 3.1 For every i, X_i is convex.

Assumption 3.2 For every i, x_i, $x_i' \in X_i$, if $x_i' <_i x_i$, then $x_i' <_i (1 - t)x_i' + tx_i$ for every $t \in (0,1)$.

Infinite time horizon

We assume that there exist normed linear spaces $\{L_t\}_{t=0}^{\infty}$ such that

$$L = \{z \equiv (z_0, z_1, \ldots) \mid z_t \in L_t \text{ for every } t \text{ and } \|z\| < \infty\},$$

where

$$\|z\| = \sup_t \|z_t\|_t$$

and $\|\cdot\|_t$ denotes the norm on L_t. Let L^n be the linear subspace of L for which $z_t = 0$ for $t \geq n$. Let z^n denote the projection of z on L^n (i.e., $z^n = (z_0, \ldots, z_n, 0, \ldots) \in L^n$). Note that L^n has the same norm as L. We introduce two more assumptions.

Assumption 3.6 For every i, $x_i \in X_i$ implies $x_i^n \in X_i$, and for every j, $y_j \in Y_j$ implies $y_j^n \in Y_j$, for every n.

Assumption 3.7 For any i, if x_i, $x_i' \in X_i$ and $x_i >_i x_i'$, then there exists an integer N such that for all $n \geq N$, $x_i^n >_i x_i'$.

Assumption 3.6 implies that the truncation of any feasible consumption (or production) plan is also feasible, and Assumption 3.7 implies that sufficiently distant consumption can be ignored while preserving the preference relationship.

Let $v(z)$be a continuous linear functional on L. Then we have:

Lemma 3.2 $P(z) \equiv \lim_{n \to \infty} v(z^n)$ exists.[8]

Proof [Prescott–Lucas (1972, p. 418)] Let $z_{(i)}$ be the sequence with the ith term equal to z_i and all other terms 0 and define z' by $z_i' = z_i$ if $v(z_{(i)}) \geq 0$ and $z_i' = -z_i$ otherwise. Then, since v is continuous, $\|v\|$ is finite, and for any n,

$$v(z'^n) = \sum_{i=0}^{n} |v(z_{(i)})| \leq \|v\| \, \|z\|.$$

Therefore, $P(z')$ exists since any bounded, monotone sequence converges. Consequently $P(z)$ also exists.   Q.E.D.

Theorem 3.3 Suppose that $[(x_i^0), (y_j^0), v]$ is a valuation equilibrium and x_i^0 is not a saturation point for any i. Then under Assumptions 3.1, 3.2, 3.6, 3.7, $[(x_i^0), (y_j^0), P]$ is a quasi-valuation equilibrium, that is,

$$\text{for every } i, \text{ if } x_i \in X_i, \ x_i \geq_i x_i^0, \text{ then } P(x_i) \geq P(x_i^0), \tag{3.5}$$

$$\text{for every } j, \text{ if } y_j \in Y_j \text{ then } P(y_j) \leq P(y_j^0), \tag{3.6}$$

and P, as defined in Lemma 3.2, is non-trivial. The quasi-valuation equilibrium $[(x_i^0), (y_j^0), P]$ is a valuation equilibrium under the conditions of Lemma 3.1 previously discussed.

Proof See Prescott–Lucas (1972, p. 418).

The use of Theorem 3.3 is that it allows one to represent a pricing scheme v as an inner product expression. To see this, let $z_{(t)}$ be a sequence with the tth term equal to z_t and all other terms 0 (i.e., $z_{(t)} = (0, \ldots, 0, z_t, 0, \ldots)$), and let $P_t(z_t) \equiv P(z_{(t)})$. Note that $z_{(t)}^n = z_{(t)}$ for $t \leq n$ and $z_{(t)}^n = 0$ for $t > n$. We want to show that

$$P(z) = \sum_{t=0}^{\infty} P_t(z_t).$$

Now

$$P(z) = \lim_{n \to \infty} v(z^n) = \lim_{n \to \infty} v\left(\sum_{t=0}^{n} z^n_{(t)}\right) \quad \left[\text{since } z^n = \sum_{t=0}^{n} z^n_{(t)}\right]$$

$$= \lim_{n \to \infty} \sum_{t=0}^{n} v(z^n_{(t)}) \qquad\qquad \text{[by linearity of } v\text{]}$$

$$= \lim_{n \to \infty} \sum_{t=0}^{n} P(z_{(t)}) \qquad\qquad \text{[for } t \leq n,\ z^n_{(t)} = z_{(t)}, \text{ and hence}$$

$$P(z_{(t)}) = \lim_{n \to \infty} v(z^n_{(t)}) = v(z_{(t)})]$$

$$= \sum_{t=0}^{\infty} P_t(z_t).$$

In particular, if L_t is a finite-dimensional Euclidean space (i.e., $L_t = \mathbf{R}^{K_t}$, $K_t < \infty$), then, since P_t is linear,

$$P_t(z_t) = p_{1t}z_{1t} + \cdots + p_{K_t t}z_{K_t t} = p'_t z_t,$$

where $z_t = (z_{1t}, \ldots, z_{K_t t})$ and $p_t = (p_{1t}, \ldots, p_{K_t t})$. Hence in this case

$$P(z) = \sum_{t=0}^{\infty} \sum_{k=1}^{K_t} p_{kt}z_{kt}.$$

The intuition for this result is that under Assumptions 3.1, 3.2, 3.6, and 3.7, the infinite-horizon economy is the limit of a sequence of finite-horizon economies, and the limit of their equilibrium price vectors is an equilibrium price vector for the infinite-horizon economy.

Uncertainty

We can achieve essentially the same result with the economic system in which the future is uncertain, with a measure-theoretic set-up. Let (Ω, Φ, P) be a probability measure space, where Ω denotes the set of possible states of the world (possibly a set of infinite sequences of realizations), and Φ is the appropriate σ-algebra of subsets of Ω, that is, the collection of eventually discernible events. Also let $\Phi_t \subset \Phi$ be the set of events that can be distinguished at date t (see Chapter 1 for a discussion of σ-algebras and their use in representing information). The probability measure $P : \Phi \to [0,1]$ gives the probability of the various events in Φ (or Φ_t).

Now we define L_t by

$L_t = \{[z_{1t}(\omega), \ldots, z_{K_t t}(\omega)] \mid z_{kt}(\omega)$ is real-valued

and Φ_t-measurable for each k, and $\|z_t\|_t < \infty\}$ for every t, where

$$\|z_t\|_t = \max_k \operatorname{ess\,sup}_{\omega \in \Omega} |z_{kt}(\omega)|.$$

$z_{kt}(\omega)$ is interpreted as the quantity of commodity k in period t if the state ω occurs (see Chapter 1 for a definition of the essential supremum). The space L is defined as previously discussed.

Since all the hypotheses of Theorem 3.3 are maintained in the uncertainty case, we know that there is an equilibrium price system $P(z)$ on L. What we are looking for is some Φ_t-measurable functions $\tilde{q}_{kt}$ such that

$$P_t(z_t) = \sum_{k=1}^{K_t} \int_\Omega \tilde{q}_{kt}(\omega) z_{kt}(\omega) P(d\omega) = \sum_{k=1}^{K_t} E[\tilde{q}_{kt} z_{kt}].$$

If A is an event in Φ_t, then

$$\int_A \tilde{q}_{kt}(\omega) P(d\omega) = E[\tilde{q}_{kt} I_A],$$

where I_A is the indicator function for the event A, is interpreted as the price (in terms of some good delivered at $t = 1$ for sure) of one unit of good k delivered at date t if the event A occurs. The $\tilde{q}_{kt}$ are referred to as "prices per unit of probability."

Next we need a notation for commodity points truncated on certain events. For $A \in \Phi_t$, with t fixed, define $z_{sk}^t(A)$, a Φ_s-measurable function on Ω, by

$$z_{ks}^t(A)(\omega) = \begin{cases} 0 & \text{if } s \geq t \text{ and } \omega \in A, \\ z_{ks}(\omega) & \text{otherwise.} \end{cases}$$

In this way we create a new consumption (or production) point from an old one by specifying that if the event A occurs, then consumption from date t on is zero. Naturally we want to make A a set of negligible probability measure. For a sequence $\{A_n\}$, $A_n \in \Phi_t$, the notation $A_n \downarrow 0$ will mean $A_n \supset A_{n+1}$ and $\lim_{n \to \infty} P(A_n) = 0$. We add two more assumptions.

Assumption 3.8   For any t, if $\{A_n\}$ is any sequence of events in Φ_t such that $A_n \downarrow 0$, and if $x_i \in X_i$ and $y_j \in Y_j$, then there exists an integer N such that for every $n \geq N$, $x_i^t(A_n) \in X_i$ and $y_j^t(A_n) \in Y_j$, where

$$x_i^t(A_n) = \{x_{is}^t(A_n)\}_{s=0}^\infty,$$
$$x_{is}^t(A_n) = [x_{i1s}^t(A_n), \ldots, x_{iK_s s}^t(A_n)],$$

$x_{iks}^t(A_n)$ is previously defined (replacing z and A with x_i and A_n, respectively), and y_j^t is also similarly defined.

Assumption 3.9 For any t and $A_n \downarrow 0$, if x_i, $x'_i \in X_i$ with $x_i >_i x'_i$, then there exists an integer N such that for every $n \geq N$, $x'_i(A_n) >_i x'_i$.

In the same spirit as Assumptions 3.6 and 3.7, Assumption 3.8 requires that conditionally truncated consumption (or production) is also feasible. Note that the truncation can be as early as you like (i.e., t can be small), provided the contingency in which the truncation occurs is sufficiently unlikely. Assumption 3.9 requires the preservation of strict preference notwithstanding the truncation, again provided the truncation probability is sufficiently small. The main result is

Theorem 3.4 Suppose that $[(x_i^0), (y_j^0), v]$ is a valuation equilibrium and x_i^0 is not a saturation point for any i. Then under Assumptions 3.1, 3.2, 3.6–3.9, $[(x_i^0), (y_j^0), Q]$ is a quasi-valuation equilibrium, that is,

$$\text{for every } i, \text{ if } x_i \in X_i, \ x_i \geq_i x_i^0, \text{ then } Q(x_i) \geq Q(x_i^0), \quad (3.7)$$

$$\text{for every } j, \text{ if } y_j \in Y_j, \text{ then } Q(y_j) \leq Q(y_j^0), \quad (3.8)$$

where

$$Q(z) = \sum_{t=0}^{\infty} \sum_{k=1}^{K_t} \int_{\Omega} \bar{q}_{kt}(\omega) z_{kt}(\omega) \, P(d\omega)$$

for some Φ_t-measurable functions $\bar{q}_{kt} : \Omega \to \mathbf{R}$, $k = 1, 2, \ldots, K_t$, $t = 1, 2, \ldots$ and $Q(\cdot)$ is non-trivial.

Proof Prescott–Lucas (1972, p. 421).

The intuition for this result is similar to that for the previous result, namely, that an economy with an infinite number of dates and states can be approximated by one with a finite number of dates and states under the given conditions.

3.3 APPLICATION: THE ONE-SECTOR EQUILIBRIUM MODEL

In this section we return to the one-sector model introduced in Chapter 2; however, we now view this model not as a vehicle for describing optimal growth relative to some planner's utility, but as an equilibrium model. The trick is to assume either that there is only one consumer, or equivalently, that all consumers are identical. We can show that the optimal allocation developed in Chapter 2 is a Pareto optimum for the equilibrium model. We can then use the tools developed in the previous two sections of this chapter to characterize the equilibrium prices. Finally, we introduce uncertainty into the analysis. The equilibrium model is as follows:

1. There is one consumer and one firm.
2. The commodity space, $L = \{x = \{x_t\}_{t=1}^{\infty} \mid x_t \in R^3 \text{ and } \|x\|_{\infty} < \infty\}$.[9]

Remember that the commodities in this formulation have a very special interpretation; they are really commodity bond contracts (not "futures" or "forward" contracts as they are often misnamed since both futures and forward contracts require no immediate payment whereas bond contracts do). That is, they are agreements entered into at date 1, in which one party (the seller) agrees to deliver a certain quantity of some good at a certain date to the other party (the buyer) in return for an immediate payment. Thus the seller is borrowing a certain amount of the good now in return for a specified payment of the good at a specified future date. Consequently, for the consumer, a point $x \in L$ has the following interpretation:

- x_{1t} is the quantity of the "consumption" good he arranges today (date 1) to have delivered and to consume at date t ("consumption" is in quotes because there is really only one physical good, but use of the adjectives "consumption" and "capital" facilitates interpretation).
- $-x_{2t}$ is the quantity of the "capital" good he agrees today to deliver to the firm *before* production at date t.
- x_{3t} is the quantity of the "capital" good he arranges today to have delivered *after* production at date t.

For the firm, a point $y \in L$ has the following interpretation:

- y_{1t} is the quantity of the "consumption" good the firm agrees today to deliver at date t.
- $-y_{2t}$ is the quantity of the "capital" good the firm arranges today to have delivered before production at date t.
- y_{3t} is the quantity of the "capital" good the firm agrees today to deliver after production at date t.

The reason for the minus signs on x_{2t} and y_{2t} is so that the equilibrium prices of these commodities will be positive (see the preceding discussion).

3. The technological constraints faced by the consumer are

$$-x_{2t} \leqslant z_t \quad \text{for all } t, \tag{3.9}$$

$$z_{t+1} = (1 - \delta)(z_t + x_{2t}) + x_{3t} \quad \text{for all } t, \tag{3.10}$$

$$z_1 = \bar{k}, \tag{3.11}$$

$$x_{1t} \geqslant 0, \quad x_{2t} \leqslant 0, \quad x_{3t} \geqslant 0, \quad z_t \geqslant 0 \quad \text{for all } t \tag{3.12}$$

for some sequence $z \in \ell_\infty$, where z_t is interpreted as the amount of capital the consumer plans to have available at t (either to sell at t or store until $t + 1$). Constraint (3.9) says that planned sales of capital cannot exceed available stocks; (3.10) says that the stock of capital available at $t + 1$ is the undepreciated portion of that part of the available stock at t that was not sold at t plus any capital purchased at $t + 1$; (3.11) says that the initial stock of capital available to the consumer is exogenously given (by $\bar{k}$); (3.12) is self-explanatory. Thus the consumption set X for the consumer is

$$X = \{x \in L \mid \text{for some } z \in \ell_\infty, \ (3.9)\text{–}(3.12) \text{ hold}\}.$$

Note that z_t is not part of the commodity point since it is not traded; z_t is simply an accounting variable for the consumer and $\{z_t\}$ is completely determined by $\bar{k}$ and $\{x_{2t}, x_{3t}\}$.

Preferences for the consumer are defined by the utility function

$$U(x) = \sum_{t=1}^{\infty} \beta^{t-1} u(x_{1t}) \quad \text{for } x \in L \text{ with } x_{1t} \geq 0 \quad \text{for all } t,$$

where $u : \mathbf{R}_+ \to \mathbf{R}$ satisfies Assumption 2.1.2 and $0 < \beta < 1$. That is, the consumer (weakly) prefers x to x' if and only if $U(x) \geq U(x')$.

4. The production possibility set Y for the firm is defined by

$$Y = \{y \in L \mid y_{1t} \geq 0, \ y_{2t} \leq 0, \ y_{3t} \geq 0, \ y_{1t} + y_{3t} \leq F(-y_{2t}) \text{ for all } t\},$$

where F is defined as in Chapter 2, and $f : \mathbf{R}_+ \to \mathbf{R}$ satisfies Assumption 2.1.1. Note that Y can be written as

$$Y = Y' \times Y' \times \dots,$$

where

$$Y' = \{(y_1, y_2, y_3) \in \mathbf{R}^3 \mid y_1, y_3 \geq 0, \ y_2 \leq 0, \ |y_i| < \infty, \ i = 1, 2, 3,$$
$$\text{and } y_1 + y_3 \leq F(-y_2)\}.$$

As in the Recursive Competitive Equilibrium framework (see Chapter 4), the firm's production possibilities in any period are unaffected by production choices of any other period. Since the firm's objective function is also time separable, the firm actually solves a static optimization problem.

5. There are no other resources in the economy, that is, the point $\zeta \in L$ defined in Section 3.1 is $\zeta = 0$.

Pareto optimality

Following Section 3.1, we say an *allocation* is a pair of points $(x, y) \in L \times L$, that is, a commodity point for the consumer and one for the firm. An allocation is *attainable* if $x \in X$, $y \in Y$, and $x = y$. An allocation is a *Pareto optimum* if there is no other attainable allocation strictly preferred by the consumer.

Thus $(x^*, y^*) \in L \times L$ is a Pareto optimum if $y^* = x^*$ and x^* solves

$$\max_{x \in X \cap Y} \sum_{t=1}^{\infty} \beta^{t-1} u(x_{1t}).$$

Given the definitions of X and Y, we can restate the foregoing problem as

$$\max_{x \in L} \sum_{t=1}^{\infty} \beta^{t-1} u(x_{1t})$$

subject to

$$-x_{2t} \leq z_t,$$

$$z_{t+1} = (1 - \delta)(z_t + x_{2t}) + x_{3t},$$

$$x_{1t} + x_{3t} \leq F(-x_{2t}),$$

$$z_t \geq 0, \quad x_{1t} \geq 0, \quad x_{2t} \leq 0, \quad x_{3t} \geq 0 \quad \text{for all } t, z_1 = \bar{k}.$$

Note that storage of capital is allowed in this problem, although it is not usually allowed in the one-sector planning problem introduced in Chapter 2. As will be seen, it is suboptimal to store capital if it depreciates as fast in storage as it does in production. It turns out that this problem is equivalent to a somewhat simpler problem. To see this, we first claim that in any solution of the problem, the consumer will sell all his available stock of capital at each date. This is intuitively obvious since keeping capital is unproductive, and the capital just depreciates at the same rate that it would depreciate if used to produce. A formal proof is left to the reader [see Exercise (3.4)]. Therefore, if the problem has a solution, the solution has the property that (3.9) is binding for all t. Hence this can be imposed as a constraint without loss of generality. Thus (3.10) implies that $-x_{2,t+1} = x_{3t}$. Letting $k_{t+1} = -x_{2,t+1} = x_{3t}$ and $c_t = x_{1t}$, we may rewrite the problem as

$$(P) \quad \max_{(c,k) \in \ell_\infty \times \ell_\infty} \sum_{t=1}^{\infty} \beta^{t-1} u(c_t)$$

subject to

$$c_t + k_{t+1} = F(k_t),$$

$$c_t \in [0, m + B], k_t \in K = [0, B] \quad \text{for all } t,$$

$$k_1 = \bar{k}.$$

This problem is exactly the optimal growth problem analyzed in Chapter 2 (the restrictions that $c_t \leq m + B$ and $k_t \leq B$ and replacement of the inequality in the first constraint with an equality were justified there). Recall that problem (P) is equivalent to problem (Q) given at the end of Chapter 2. It was also shown that a unique solution to (Q) exists and the following general properties of the solution were derived.

First, the optimality equation for (Q),

$$v^*(k) = \max_{F(k) \geq c \geq 0} u(c) + \beta v^*[F(k) - c], \tag{3.13}$$

has a unique solution v^* that is continuous, strictly increasing, and strictly concave (Lemma 2.8), and the maximization problem on the right-hand side has a unique solution, $g(k)$, that is continuous (Lemma 2.9). Moreover, v^* is differentiable on $(0, B)$, $v^{*\prime} > 0$, $v^{*\prime}$ is strictly decreasing, and for $k \in (0, B)$ such that $g(k) > 0$,

$$v^{*\prime}(k) = u'[g(k)]F'(k).$$

We also showed that g is monotone increasing and $h(k) = F(k) - g(k)$ is also monotone increasing (Lemma 2.10 and Exercise 2.11). Finally, we showed that the optimal paths of the capital stock $\{k_t^*\}$ and consumption $\{c_t^*\}$ are monotone and converge to k^* satisfying $f'(k^*) = \rho + \delta$ (or $F'(k^*) = 1/\beta = 1 + \rho$), where $\rho = (1/\beta) - 1$, and $c^* = F(k^*) - k^*$ (Theorem 2.6 and Exercise 2.12).

Valuation equilibrium

The next step in characterizing a competitive equilibrium is to apply Theorem 3.2 and to verify that the hypotheses of Lemma 3.1 also hold, so that we are assured of the existence of a valuation equilibrium.

To apply Theorem 3.2, we must verify that Assumptions 3.1–3.5 hold. These are verified as follows [recall the definitions of X and Y and the single consumer's preferences $U(\cdot)$]:

Assumption 3.1.   Obviously, X is convex.

Assumption 3.2.   See Exercise 3.5.

Assumption 3.3.   By Exercise 3.1, it suffices to show that U is continuous in the norm-topology on L. Let $\varepsilon > 0$ be given. Since u is continuous, we can choose $\delta > 0$ such that $|c - c'| < \delta$ implies that $|u(c) - u(c')| < \varepsilon(1 - \beta)$. Now if $x, x' \in X$ and $\|x - x'\|_\infty < \delta$, then $|x_{1t} - x'_{1t}| < \delta$ for every t. Therefore,

$$|U(x) - U(x')| < \varepsilon(1 - \beta) \sum_{t=1}^{\infty} \beta^{t-1} = \varepsilon.$$

Assumption 3.4.   See Exercise 3.6.

Assumption 3.5.   Let k' be any number such that $0 < k' < \hat{k}$ and $k' \leqslant \bar{k}$ (clearly such a k' exists since $\hat{k} > 0$ and $\bar{k} > 0$). Define y by

$$-y_{2t} = y_{3t} = k' \quad \text{and} \quad y_{1t} = \tfrac{1}{2}[f(k') - \delta k'] \quad \text{for every } t.$$

It can be shown that y is an interior point of Y (see Exercise 3.7). That there are no saturation points in X follows from monotonicity of u (see Exercise 3.7).

Now by Theroem 3.2, if $\{c_t^*, k_t^*\}$ solves problem (P), then, letting

$$x_{1t}^* = y_{1t}^* = c_t^*, \quad -x_{2t}^* = -y_{2t}^* = k_t^*, \quad \text{and} \quad x_{3t}^* = y_{3t}^* = k_{t+1}^*$$

for every t, there is a non-trivial linear form $v(\cdot)$ on L such that

if $x \in X$ and $U(x) \geq U(x^*)$, then $v(x) \geq v(x^*)$, (3.14)

if $y \in Y$, then $v(y) \leq v(y^*)$. (3.15)

In order that v represent a valuation equilibrium, we must show that there is an $x' \in X$ such that $v(x') < v(x^*)$. But $0 \in X$ [here $0 = ((0,0,0), (0,0,0), \ldots)$] and $v(0) = 0$ since v is linear. But $0 \in Y$, so by (3.15), $v(x^*) = v(y^*) \geq v(0) = 0$. If $v(x^*) > 0$, we are done since we may take $x' = 0$. If $v(x^*) = v(y^*) = 0$ and if there is $x' \in X$ such that $v(x') < 0$, we are also done. So suppose $v(x^*) = v(y^*) = 0$ and for all $x \in X$, $v(x) \geq 0$. Now by (3.15), $v(y) \leq 0$ all $y \in Y$. Thus for all $x \in X \cap Y$, $v(x) = 0$. But we claim that $\text{Int}(X \cap Y) \neq \emptyset$. In particular, let $k' = \frac{1}{2}\min(\hat{k}, \bar{k})$. Then x^0 defined by

$$z_1^0 = \bar{k}, \quad z_{t+1}^0 = (1 - \delta)(z_t^0 + x_{2t}^0) + x_{3t}^0,$$
$$-x_{2t}^0 = k', \quad x_{1t}^0 = [f(k') - \delta k']/2 \equiv Q/2,$$
$$x_{3t}^0 = [f(k') - \delta k']/4 + k' = Q/4 + k'$$

is in the $\text{Int}(X \cap Y)$. The intuition for this is as follows. We choose k' to be less than the maximum sustainable capital stock $\hat{k}$ and less than the initial stock $\bar{k}$. Therefore, this level of capital stock can be maintained with some output left over. The firm chooses to sell consumption goods equal to one-half the amount left over after maintaining the capital stock. Half of the other half is sold back to consumers along with the capital stock used that period, k', at the end of the period. Thus the stock available to consumers exceeds k' at each date. Nevertheless, consumers only sell k' to the firm each period. This allocation results in slack so that all traded quantities can be increased or decreased slightly without violating any constraints. To construct a formal proof, choose $\varepsilon > 0$ such that

$$\varepsilon \leq \min\{k', Q/8\}$$

and

$$\tfrac{3}{4}F(k') + \tfrac{1}{4}k' + 2\varepsilon \leq F(k' - \varepsilon).$$

It is easy to check that such an ε exists (see Exercise 3.8) and that if x is such that $\|x - x^0\|_\infty < \varepsilon$, then $x \in X \cap Y$ (see Exercise 3.9). Now $\text{Int}(X \cap Y) \neq \emptyset$ and is open (in L) and $v \equiv 0$ on $\text{Int}(X \cap Y)$. I claim that this implies that v is trivial, for suppose $x \in L$. Let $x' \in \text{Int}(X \cap Y)$ and $\varepsilon > 0$ be such that for any $x'' \in L$ with $\|x'' - x'\|_\infty < \varepsilon$, $x'' \in \text{Int}(X \cap Y)$. Also let $M = \|x - x'\|_\infty < \infty$. Choose $\lambda > 0$ such that $\lambda M < \varepsilon$, and let $y = x' + \lambda(x - x')$. Now $\|y - x'\|_\infty = \lambda \|x - x'\|_\infty = \lambda M < \varepsilon$ so $v(y) = 0$. But $v(y) = v(x') + \lambda v(x) - \lambda v(x') = \lambda v(x)$ since $v(x') = 0$. Therefore, $v(x) = 0$ since

$\lambda > 0$. This shows that v is trivial in contradiction of our result that v is nontrivial. Therefore, either $v(x^*) > 0$ or $v(x^*) = 0$ and there is $x' \in X$ such that $v(x') < 0$. In either case we are done.

Next we must show that v can be represented as a sequence of prices $p = \{p_t\} \in L$. We also want to show that $p_{it} > 0$ for $i = 1, 2, 3$ and every t, and several other properties of these prices. To do this, we will apply Theorem 3.3 and hence must verify Assumptions 3.1, 3.2, 3.6, and 3.7. Assumptions 3.1 and 3.2 have already been verified. Assumption 3.6 is obvious. Assumption 3.7 is verified in Exercise 3.2.

Now letting $x^* = y^*$ and v be as defined above, Theorem 3.3 implies that there is a non-trivial continuous linear functional Q on L such that

$$\text{if } x \in X \text{ and } U(x) \geq U(x^*), \text{ then } Q(x) \geq Q(x^*), \tag{3.16}$$

$$\text{if } y \in Y, \text{ then } Q(y) \leq Q(y^*). \tag{3.17}$$

Moreover, Q can be represented as $p = \{p_t\} \in L$, where $p_t = (p_{1t}, p_{2t}, p_{3t})$ for each t (this follows from the fact that $L_t = \mathbf{R}^3$ so the dual $L_t^* = \mathbf{R}^3$ for each t as shown in Chapter 1), that is,

$$Q(z) = pz = \sum_{t=1}^{\infty} p_t z_t \quad \text{for any } z \in L.$$

It can also be shown that there is a point $x' \in X$ such that $Q(x') < Q(x^*)$ by an argument identical to the one for v given earlier. Thus, $[x^*, y^*, Q]$ is a valuation equilibrium. This argument also shows that $px^* = py^* \geq 0$.

Since $[x^*, y^*, Q]$ is a valuation equilibrium, we have that y^* solves

$$(F) \quad \max_{y \in L} \sum_{t=1}^{\infty} [p_{1t} y_{1t} + p_{2t} y_{2t} + p_{3t} y_{3t}]$$

subject to

$$y_{1t} \geq 0, \quad y_{2t} \leq 0, \quad y_{3t} \geq 0,$$

$$y_{1t} + y_{3t} \leq F(-y_{2t}) \quad \text{for each } t, \tag{3.18}$$

that is, y^* is a profit maximizing production plan where prices p are taken as given. Using standard Lagrange multiplier methods on this problem (since each y_{it} appears in only one term in the objective function and two contemporaneous constraints, the problem can be decomposed into a sequence of one-period problems) yields the following first-order conditions for a solution with $y_{1t} > 0$, $y_{2t} < 0$, and $y_{3t} > 0$:

$$p_{1t} = \lambda_t, \tag{3.19}$$

$$p_{2t} = \lambda_t[f'(-y_{2t}) + 1 - \delta], \tag{3.20}$$

$$p_{3t} = \lambda_t, \tag{3.21}$$

which must hold for each t, where $\lambda_t \geq 0$ is a Lagrange multiplier associated with the tth constraint in (3.18).

Henceforth we assume that $u'(0) = \infty$ so that $y_{1t}^* > 0$, $y_{2t}^* < 0$, $y_{3t}^* > 0$ for each t. Therefore, (3.20) must hold for $y_{2t} = y_{2t}^* = -k_t^*$, and (3.19) and (3.21) must also hold. Consequently, for each t,

$$p_{3t} = p_{1t}, \tag{3.22}$$

$$p_{2t} = p_{1t}[1 + \rho_t], \tag{3.23}$$

where ρ_t is defined by $1 + \rho_t = F'(k_t^*)$. Equation (3.22) says that the firm must be indifferent between selling its output as capital or as consumption in period t. Since the rate of transformation between the two goods is constant at one, if the firm were not indifferent, then either no consumption good would be sold or no capital good would be sold for period t delivery. The equilibrium quantities are, however, positive. To interpret equation (3.23), note that a little extra capital purchased for date t delivery yields output of $F'(k_t^*)$, which can be sold at p_{1t} (or equivalently at p_{3t}). Equation (3.23) says that the revenue generated by this just equals the cost of the extra capital, p_{2t}. Note that $\rho_t \to \rho = (1/\beta) - 1$ since f' is continuous and $k_t \to k^*$, where $k^* \in (0, \hat{k})$ is such that $h(k^*) = k^*$.

Also since $[x^*, y^*, Q]$ is a valuation equilibrium, x^* solves

$$(C) \quad \max_{x \in L} \sum_{t=1}^{\infty} \beta^{t-1} u(x_{1t})$$

subject to

$$x_{1t} \geq 0, \quad x_{2t} \leq 0, \quad x_{3t} \geq 0, \quad -x_{2,t+1} \leq x_{3t} \quad \text{for all } t,$$
$$-x_{21} \leq \bar{k},$$

and

$$\sum_{t=1}^{\infty} [p_{1t}x_{1t} + p_{2t}x_{2t} + p_{3t}x_{3t}] \leq px^*, \tag{3.24}$$

taking p as given.

Again using standard Lagrange multiplier techniques and letting $\gamma_t \geq 0$ be the multiplier for $-x_{2,t+1} \leq x_{3t}$ (or $0 \leq x_{3t} + x_{2,t+1}$) and $\gamma \geq 0$ be the multiplier for (3.24), any solution with $x_{1t} > 0$, $x_{2t} < 0$, $x_{3t} > 0$ for each t must satisfy, for each t,

$$\beta^{t-1} u'(x_{1t}) = \gamma p_{1t}, \tag{3.25}$$

$$\gamma_{t-1} = \gamma p_{2t}, \tag{3.26}$$

$$\gamma_t = \gamma p_{3t}. \tag{3.27}$$

Again x^* is a solution with $x_{1t}^* > 0$, $x_{2t}^* < 0$, $x_{3t}^* > 0$ for every t so (3.25) must hold with $x_{1t} = x_{1t}^* = c_t^*$ for each t and (3.26) and (3.27) must also hold for each t. Therefore, from (3.26) and (3.27),

$$p_{3t} = p_{2,t+1}. \tag{3.28}$$

Combining (3.28), (3.22), and (3.23) yields

$$p_{1t} = p_{3t} = p_{2,t+1} = p_{1,t+1}(1 + \rho_{t+1})$$

or

$$\frac{p_{1t}}{p_{1,t+1}} = 1 + \rho_{t+1} = \frac{p_{2,t+1}}{p_{1,t+1}} = \frac{p_{3t}}{p_{1,t+1}}. \tag{3.29}$$

From (3.29) we see that consumption goods delivered one period later are cheaper by a factor of $1/(1 + \rho_{t+1})$. Note that ρ_{t+1} may be interpreted as the one-period forward interest rate between periods t and $t+1$ since $1 + \rho_{t+1}$ is the price of period t consumption in terms of period $t+1$ consumption. In the steady-state, this one-period interest rate converges to $\rho = 1/\beta - 1 = f'(k^*) - \delta$ = steady-state marginal product of capital net of depreciation. Also in any period ρ_t is the marginal product of capital net of depreciation. Also using (3.25) and (3.29),

$$1 + \rho_{t+1} = \frac{p_{1t}}{p_{1,t+1}} = \frac{1}{\beta} \frac{u'(c_t^*)}{u'(c_{t+1}^*)}, \tag{3.30}$$

that is, the relative price of consumption in any two periods is the marginal rate of substitution between consumption in those periods.

Next, note that if x^* and y^* solve the consumer and firm problems (C) and (F) above given p, then they also solve these problems given αp, where α is any positive real number. Now claim that $p_{11} > 0$ for suppose not. If $p_{11} = 0$, then by (3.29), $p_{1t} = 0$ for all t and so by (3.22) and (3.23), $p_{2t} = p_{3t} = 0$ for all t. But this is impossible since Q is non-trivial and p represents Q. Moreover, if $p_{11} < 0$, then $p_{it} < 0$ for $i = 1, 2, 3$ and all t since $\rho_t > 0$. In this case $px^* < 0$ (see Exercise 3.10). This is a contradiction (see above). Therefore, $p_{11} > 0$. Let $\alpha = 1/p_{11}$. Then αp is also a competitive equilibrium price sequence with the price of consumption in period one being unity. This shows that $p_{it} > 0$ for all t and $i = 1, 2, 3$ and that we may assume, without loss of generality that $p_{11} = 1$.

Herewith, a few parting shots relating to this equilibrium:

1. If we define new prices by $p_t' = p_t/\beta^{t-1}$, then by (3.30), $p_{1t}'/p_{1,t+1}' \to 1$,

$$\frac{p_{2t}'}{p_{2,t+1}'} = \beta \frac{p_{2t}}{p_{2,t+1}} = \beta \frac{p_{2t}}{p_{1t}} \frac{p_{1t}}{p_{1,t+1}} \frac{p_{1,t+1}}{p_{2,t+1}} \to \beta(1/\beta)(1/\beta)\beta = 1$$

and

$$\frac{p_{3t}'}{p_{3,t+1}'} = \frac{p_{2,t+1}'}{p_{2,t+2}'} \to 1,$$

that is, the "undiscounted" prices p' converge to a steady state. Since the actual prices are of the form $p_t = \beta^t p_t'$, and β^t approaches zero as t approaches infinity, this implies that $p_t \to 0$.

2. The value of the equilibrium allocation $x^* = y^*$ at the equilibrium prices is

$$px^* = \sum_{t=1}^{\infty} p_{1t}c_t^* - p_{21}\bar{k},$$

that is, it is the value of the consumption output net of the value of the initial resources. This is, of course, also the value of the firm in this model (see Exercise 3.11).

3. The competitive equilibrium price system depends on the initial capital stock $\bar{k}$ since ρ_t depends on k_t^*, which in turn depends on $\bar{k}$.

4. Finally, the firm's value maximization problem (F) is not really a dynamic problem, that is, it can be solved as a sequence of one-period static maximization problems. This follows from the fact that there are no relationships in the profit function or in the equations defining the constraint set between y_t and $y_{t'}$ for $t \neq t'$. This in turn follows from the way in which the commodity space is defined.

One-sector equilibrium model with uncertainty

In this section, we introduce uncertainty into the one-sector model. This is accomplished by assuming that the output of the single good in any given period is a random variable whose distribution depends on the capital services employed in that period. We then apply the techniques discussed in Sections 3.1 and 3.2 to this model and analyze the competitive equilibrium prices and quantities. Although the development is formally similar to that for the certainty case, the interpretation of the equilibrium is quite different.

To begin, we assume that output at any time t is given by

$$\tilde{Q}_t = f(k_t, \bar{r}_t) + (1 - \delta)k_t \equiv F(k_t, \bar{r}_t),$$

where $\{\bar{r}_t\}$ is an i.i.d. sequence of real-valued random variables and f satisfies Assumption 2.1.1 with respect to its first argument for each value of its second argument. A realization r_t of $\bar{r}_t$ is interpreted as the "state of nature at date t." We further assume

Assumption 3.10

1. f is differentiable and strictly increasing with respect to its second argument.
2. The support of $\bar{r}_t$ is $[a,b]$, where $0 < a < b < \infty$.

Let v be the measure associated with $\tilde{r}_t$, that is, if B is any Borel subset of the real line, then

$$v(B) = \Pr[\tilde{r}_t \in B]. \tag{3.31}$$

Finally, we assume that the period utility function, u, of our single consumer satisfies Assumption 2.1.2.

Now, let (Ω, Φ, P) be the probability space underlying the $\{\tilde{r}_t\}$ process, that is,

$\Omega = [a,b] \times [a,b] \times \cdots,$

Φ is the σ-algebra of subsets of Ω generated by cylinder sets of the form $B_1 \times B_2 \times \cdots \times B_t \times \cdots$, where B_t is a Borel subset of $[a,b]$ and $B_t = [a,b]$ for all but a finite number of values of t,

P is a probability measure defined on Φ such that for any Borel subset B of $[a,b]$, $v(B) = P\{\prod_{s=1}^{t-1}[a,b] \times B \times \prod_{s=t+1}^{\infty}[a,b]\}.$

Thus $\tilde{r}_t(\omega) = \omega_t = r_t$.

We may now define the commodity space of our economy as in Section 3.1. Let $\{\Phi_t\}$ be the filtration generated by the history of the $\{\tilde{r}_t\}$ process, that is, Φ_t is the σ-algebra of subsets of Ω generated by sets of the form $\prod_{s=1}^{\infty} B_s$, where B_s is a Borel subset of $[a,b]$ and $B_s = [a,b]$ for $s > t$. Define the period-t commodity space by

$$L_t = \{x_t : \Omega \to \mathbf{R}^3 \mid x_{it} \text{ is } \Phi_t\text{-measurable}, i = 1, 2, 3, \text{ and } \|x_t\|_t < \infty\},$$

where

$$\|x_t\|_t = \max_i \operatorname*{ess\,sup}_{\omega \in \Omega} |x_t(\omega)|,$$

and

$$L = \{x = (x_1, x_2, \ldots) \mid x_t \in L_t \text{ for every } t \text{ and } \|x\| < \infty\},$$

where

$$\|x\| = \sup_t \|x_t\|_t.$$

The interpretation of the x_{it} are the same as in the certainty case except that now each quantity $x_{it}(\omega)$ is interpreted as the amount delivered if and only if the "state of the world" is ω. Note that x_{it} is assumed to be Φ_t-measurable so that all agents can tell at date t which value of x_{it} is correct (even though they cannot tell which ω has occurred). As in the certainty case, we will denote by y_{it} the corresponding goods from the point of view of the firm.

The technological constraints faced by the consumer are the same as (3.9)–(3.12) except that now these constraints need only hold with probability one (or almost surely), that is, there exists $z \in L'$ (where L' is the same as L except that the components z_t have range $\mathbf{R}$ instead of $\mathbf{R}^3$)

such that

$$-x_{2t} \leq z_t \text{ for all } t \text{ and almost surely (a.s.),} \qquad (3.32)$$

$$z_{t+1} = (1 - \delta)(z_t + x_{2t}) + x_{3t} \text{ for all } t \text{ and a.s.,} \qquad (3.33)$$

$$z_1 = \bar{k}, \qquad (3.34)$$

$$x_{1t} \geq 0, \quad x_{2t} \leq 0, \quad x_{3t} \geq 0, \quad z_t \geq 0, \quad \text{all } t \text{ and a.s.,} \qquad (3.35)$$

where $z_t(\omega)$ is interpreted as the amount of capital the consumer plans to have available at t in state of the world ω. The consumer's consumption set is thus

$$X = \{x \in L \mid \text{for some } z \in L', (3.32)\text{–}(3.35) \text{ hold}\}.$$

Preferences of the consumer are

$$U(x) = E \sum_{t=1}^{\infty} \beta^{t-1} u[x_{1t}(\omega)]. \qquad (3.36)$$

The production possibilities set Y for the firm is also defined exactly as in the certainty case except, again, all constraints need hold only a.s. As before the point $\zeta \in L$ is the null vector, that is, $\zeta(\omega) = 0$ a.s.

It can be shown that (see Exercise 3.14) the Pareto problem for this economy can be written as

$$(\tilde{P}) \quad \max_{(c,k)\in L'\times L'} \quad E \sum_{t=1}^{\infty} \beta^{t-1} u[c_t(\omega)]$$

subject to

$$c_t + k_{t+1} = F(k_t, r_t), \quad \text{all } t \geq 1, \quad \text{a.s.}$$

$$c_t \in [0, B + m], \quad k_t \in K = [0, B], \quad \text{all } t \geq 1, \quad \text{a.s.}$$

$$k_1 = \bar{k},$$

where L' is defined in the preceding discussion and

$$B = \max(\hat{k} + m, \bar{k}),$$

$$\hat{k} = \max_r \hat{k}(r) = \hat{k}(b),$$

$$m = \max_r m(r),$$

$\hat{k}(r)$ is the unique solution of $f(k,r) = \delta k$ (or $F(k,r) = k$),

$$m(r) = \max_k f(k,r) - \delta k.$$

Note that $\hat{k}(r)$ and $m(r)$ exist and are continuous by Assumption 2.1.1. Since $r \in [a,b]$, $\hat{k}$ and m exist.

This problem can be formulated as a dynamic program by taking the state space to be $K \times [a,b]$ and the action space to be $[0, m + B]$. The law of motion is

$$dq(k',r' \mid k,r,c) = \begin{cases} v(dr') & \text{if } k' = F(k,r) - c \\ 0 & \text{otherwise.} \end{cases}$$

The optimality equation is thus

$$v^*(k,r) = \max_{F(k,r) \geqslant c \geqslant 0} u(c) + \beta \int_a^b v^*[F(k,r) - c, r']v(dr'). \qquad (3.37)$$

As in the certainty case, we have

Lemma 3.3 The optimality equation (3.37) has a unique solution v^* that is continuous and strictly increasing in both arguments and strictly concave in the first argument.

Proof The problem satisfies all the properties assumed for stationary, discounted, dynamic programming problems in Chapter 2 (since the state space is compact). Therefore, by Theorem 2.2, a solution v^* of (3.37) exists and

$$v^* = \lim_{n \to \infty} U^n v,$$

where U is the operator defined by (3.37) as in Chapter 2. The proof of continuity, monotonicity, and concavity of v^* is very similar to the certainty case (see Lemma 2.8) and is omitted.   Q.E.D.

Lemma 3.4 Problem $(\bar{P})$ has a unique, continuous optimal policy, $g : K \times [a,b] \to [0, m + B]$.

Proof Since v^* and F are continuous, the integral in (3.37) is continuous with respect to c, k, and r. Since u is continuous and the correspondence $(k,r) \to [0, F(k,r)]$ is continuous (Theorem 1.2), Corollary 2.1 implies that the maximization problem in (3.37) has a solution. Since u is strictly concave, v^* is strictly concave in its first argument, and $[0, F(k,r)]$ is compact and convex, the solution, $g(k,r)$ is unique. Therefore, by Corollary 2.1, g is continuous. Finally, by Theorem 2.3, g is the unique optimal policy for problem $(\bar{P})$.   Q.E.D.

It is clear from (3.37) that g depends on (k,r) only through output, $F(k,r)$, that is, $g(k,r) = \hat{g}(F(k,r))$ for some $\hat{g} : \mathbf{R} \to \mathbf{R}$. Also if $h(k,r)$ is the optimal capital stock for next period as a function of this period's stock and state of nature, then

$$h(k,r) = F(k,r) - g(k,r) \equiv \hat{h}(F(k,r)).$$

To derive the properties of the optimal policy, we must first obtain a formula for the marginal value of an extra unit of capital, that is, for v_1^*.

Theorem 3.5 The function v^* is differentiable with respect to k on $(0,B)$, $v_1^* > 0$, v_1^* is strictly decreasing in k for any (k,r) and for any $k \in (0,B)$ such that $g(k,r) > 0$,

$$v_1^*(k,r) = u'[g(k,r)]F_1(k,r). \tag{3.38}$$

Proof The proof exactly parallels that of Theorem 2.5 and is omitted.

The first-order condition for an interior maximum of the problem defined in the optimality equation is now

$$u'(c) = \beta \int_a^b v_1^*[F(k,r) - c, r']v(dr'). \tag{3.39}$$

Since v_1^* is decreasing in its first argument and u' is decreasing, it is clear that the solution of (3.39) is strictly increasing in $Q = F(k,r)$. Thus whenever $\hat{g}(Q)$ is interior, $\hat{g}$ is strictly increasing. Since F is strictly increasing in both arguments, $g(k,r) = \hat{g}(F(k,r))$ is also strictly increasing in both arguments whenever $g(k,r)$ is interior. It can also be shown (as in Exercise 2.11) that $\hat{h}$ is strictly increasing and hence h is strictly increasing in both arguments. These results are summarized in

Lemma 3.5 The optimal policies g and h are strictly increasing in both arguments whenever (k,r) are such that $0 < g(k,r) < F(k,r)$.

Recall that in the deterministic case, the optimal capital stock and consumption converged to steady-state values as t approached infinity. In the present model, the analogous behavior is that the capital stock converges to a steady-state *distribution*. More precisely, suppose that for any Borel set B,

$$\mu_t(B) = \Pr\{k_t^* \in B\}, \tag{3.40}$$

where k_t^* is the optimal capital stock at date t (which is determined by the optimal policy g as a function of the state of the world ω). Let M_t be the distribution function associated with μ_t, that is,

$$M_t(k) = \mu_t([0,k)).$$

Since the optimal policy is stationary and $\{\tilde{r}_t\}$ is i.i.d., the $\{k_t^*\}$ process is Markovian. Let

$$P(k,B) = \Pr\{k_{t+1}^* \in B \mid k_t^* = k\} \tag{3.41}$$

for any Borel set B. Then

$$P(k,B) = \Pr\{h(k,r) \in B\} = v(B_k), \tag{3.42}$$

where
$$B_k = \{r \mid h(k,r) \in B\}. \tag{3.43}$$

We may now write μ_t and M_t recursively as

$$\mu_t(B) = \int_K P(k,B)\mu_{t-1}(dk) \tag{3.44}$$

and

$$M_t(k) = \int_K P(x,[0,k))\, dM_{t-1}(x). \tag{3.45}$$

With this notation, we can define a *steady-state measure* μ, and its associated *steady-state distribution*, M, by

$$\mu(B) = \int_K P(k,B)\mu(dk) \quad \text{for any Borel set } B \tag{3.46}$$

and

$$M(k) = \int_K P(x,[0,k))\, dM(x) = \mu([0,k)). \tag{3.47}$$

It can be shown that steady-state distributions exist for this problem. Since the proofs are long and tedious, we will not reproduce them here. Instead, we will attempt to summarize the results of the literature. Some examples are contained in the exercises at the end of this chapter. First we state some additional assumptions that are used in these results.

Assumption 3.11 $F_1(0,r) = \infty$, $F_1(\infty,r) = 0$ for all r.

Assumption 3.12 $u'(0) = \infty$.

Theorem 3.6 [Brock and Mirman (1972), Theorem 4.1, p. 507].   Under Assumptions 2.1 and 3.10–3.12, a unique stable distribution M exists that is independent of initial capital and $M_t \to M$ as $t \to \infty$. Moreover, if k_M is the largest fixed point of $h(k,a)$ and k_m is the smallest fixed point of $h(k,b)$, then k_M and $k_m \in K$ exist, $k_m > k_M$, and the support of M is contained in $[k_M, k_m]$. See Figure 3.6, which is adapted from Brock and Mirman (1972, Figure 5, p. 496).

This result has been extended to the case where F is not monotone in r by Mirman and Zilcha (1975). A slightly simpler proof is given in Mirman (1973) for situations in which the function h has certain additional properties. In this case, M is shown to have a density function. A nice survey is provided in Mirman (1980).

We conclude this chapter by proving existence of a competitive equilibrium for the one-sector model with uncertainty. This is done by

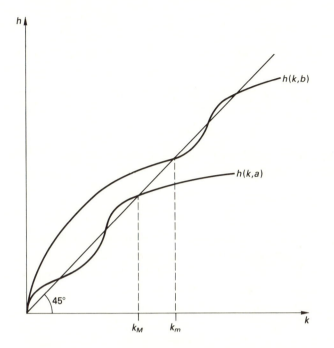

Fig. 3.6 Support of the steady-state capital stock distribution.

invoking Theorems 3.2 and 3.4. Therefore, we must verify Assumptions 3.1–3.9.

Assumption 3.1. See Exercise 3.15.

Assumption 3.2. See Exercise 3.15.

Assumption 3.3. By Exercise 3.1, it suffices to show that U as defined in (3.36) is continuous in the norm-topology on L. Suppose $\{x^n\}$ is a sequence in L and $x^n \to x$ as $n \to \infty$. Choose $\varepsilon > 0$. By continuity of u, there is a $\delta > 0$ such that if $|c - c'| < \delta$, then $|u(c) - u(c')| < \varepsilon(1 - \beta)$. Since $x^n \to x$, we can choose N such that for all $n > N$,

$$\|x_{1t}^n - x_{1t}\|_t < \delta \quad \text{for all } t. \tag{3.48}$$

Now

$$|U(x^n) - U(x)| \le \sum_{t=1}^{\infty} \beta^{t-1} \int_{\Omega} |u(x_{1t}^n(\omega)) - u(x_{1t}(\omega))| \, P(d\omega)$$

by the triangle inequality, and since, by definition of L, both the sum and integral exist. But by (3.48), for all $n > N$,

$$|x_{1t}^n - x_{1t}| < \delta \quad \text{for all } t \text{ and a.s.}$$

Therefore, for $n > N$,

$$|u(x^n_{1t}) - u(x_{1t})| < \varepsilon(1 - \beta) \quad \text{for all } t \text{ and a.s.,}$$

and, so, for $n > N$,

$$|U(x^n) - U(x)| < \sum_{t=1}^{\infty} \beta^{t-1}\varepsilon(1 - \beta) = \varepsilon.$$

Assumption 3.4. See Exercise 3.15.

Assumption 3.5. By Assumption 2.1.1, we can choose $0 < k' < \hat{k}(a)$ and $k' < \bar{k}$. Define y by

$$-y_{2t}(\omega) = y_{3t}(\omega) = k' \quad \text{for all } t \text{ and } \omega, \tag{3.49}$$

$$y_{1t}(\omega) = [f(k',a) - \delta k']/2 \quad \text{for all } t \text{ and } \omega. \tag{3.50}$$

Thus y consists of maintaining capital stock k' forever, consuming one-half of the new net output of the worst technology, and throwing the rest away. By choice of k', $[f(k',a) - \delta k']/2 > 0$. It can be shown (see Exercise 3.16) that $y \in Y$ and there exists $k' > \varepsilon > 0$ such that

$$[f(k',a) - \delta k']/2 + k' + 2\varepsilon < F(k' - \varepsilon, a) \tag{3.51}$$

and

$$2\varepsilon < f(k',a) - \delta k'. \tag{3.52}$$

It is easy to verify that the nonnegativity and nonpositivity constraints of Y hold for any y' such that $\|y' - y\| < \varepsilon$ (see Exercise 3.16).

Now if $\|y' - y\| < \varepsilon$, then for all t,

$$\begin{aligned}
y'_{1t} + y'_{3t} &< y_{1t} + y_{3t} + 2\varepsilon \quad \text{a.s.} \\
&= [f(k',a) - \delta k']/2 + k' + 2\varepsilon \\
&< F(k' - \varepsilon, a) \quad \text{by} \quad (3.51) \\
&\leq F(-y'_{2t}, a) \\
&\leq F(-y'_{2t}, r_t) \quad \text{for any } r_t \in [a,b].
\end{aligned}$$

Thus the open ball of radius ε centered at y is contained in Y.

Since it is easy to check that X contains no saturation points (see Exercise 3.17), we are ready to prove

Theorem 3.7 The point $x^* = y^*$ defined by

$$x^*_{1t}(\omega) = c^*_t(\omega),$$

$$-x^*_{2t}(\omega) = x^*_{3,t-1}(\omega) = k^*_t(\omega),$$

where c^*_t and k^*_t are defined recursively by

$$c^*_t(\omega) = g(k^*_t(\omega), \omega_t),$$

$$k^*_{t+1}(\omega) = h(k^*_t(\omega), \omega_t),$$

and g and h are the optimal policy functions for problem $(\tilde{P})$ as previously defined (see Lemma 3.4 and following discussion), can be supported as a valuation equilibrium by a non-trivial, continuous, linear functional v on L.

Proof That $x^* = y^*$ can be supported as a quasi-valuation equilibrium by a non-trivial, continuous, linear functional v on L is immediate from Theorem 3.2. Also, it can be shown, using an argument almost identical to that used for the certainty case, that there is $x \in X$ such that $v(x) < v(x^*)$. Thus by Lemma 3.1, v is a valuation equilibrium.   Q.E.D.

To show that v can be represented as prices, we must verify Assumptions 3.6–3.9.

Assumptions 3.6 and 3.7 are verified in Exercise 3.18. To verify Assumptions 3.8 and 3.9, let t be fixed but arbitrary, and let $\{A_n\}$ be a sequence of events in Φ_t with $A_n \downarrow 0$. Also let $x, x' \in X$ and $y \in Y$.

Assumption 3.8. We can show that this holds for any n (even if $P(A_n)$ is not small). It is easy to verify that the sequence defined by $z'_1 = \bar{k}$, and for $s \geq 1$,

$$z'_{s+1} = (1 - \delta)(z'_s + x^t_{2s}(A_n)) + x^t_{3s}(A_n)$$

is such that $x^t(A_n)$ satisfies (3.32)–(3.35). It is similarly easy to verify that $y^t(A_n) \in Y$.

Assumption 3.9. Suppose $U(x) > U(x')$. Choose N such that for all $n > N$,

$$P(A_n) < \frac{(1 - \beta)[U(x) - U(x')]}{\beta^{t-1}[u(B + m) - u(0)]}.$$

Then

$$U[x^t(A_n)] = U(x) - \sum_{s=t}^{\infty} \beta^{s-1} \int_{A_n} [u(x_s) - u(0)]P(d\omega)$$

$$\geq U(x) - \sum_{s=t}^{\infty} \beta^{s-1}[u(B + m) - u(0)]P(A_n)$$

$$> U(x) - [U(x) - U(x')](1 - \beta) \sum_{s=t}^{\infty} \beta^{s-t}$$

$$= U(x) - [U(x) - U(x')]$$

$$= U(x').$$

Theorem 3.8 There is a non-trivial, continuous, linear functional Q such that $[x^*, y^*, Q]$ is a valuation equilibrium, where $x^* = y^*$ are defined in

Theorem 3.7, and

$$Q(x) = \sum_{t=1}^{\infty} q_t(x_t),$$

$$q_t(x_t) = \sum_{i=1}^{3} E[\tilde{q}_{it} x_{it}]$$

for some $\tilde{q}_{it} \in L_t$.

Proof That $x^* = y^*$ can be supported as a quasi-valuation equilibrium by a q of the given form follows from Theorem 3.4. That $[x^*, y^*, Q]$ is a valuation equilibrium follows from Lemma 3.1 since Q has the same properties used to show that there is $x \in X$ such that $v(x) < v(x^*)$.

Q.E.D.

This concludes our analysis of the one-sector model.

EXERCISES

3.1. Suppose i's preference ordering can be represented by $U_i : L \rightarrow \mathbf{R}$, where U_i is continuous in the norm-topology on L. Show that Assumption 3.3 is satisfied.

3.2. Show that $\sum_{t=1}^{\infty} \beta^t u(c_t)$ satisfies Assumption 3.7.

3.3. Suppose the state of an economy is specified by an infinite sequence $\omega = (\lambda_1, \lambda_2, \ldots)$, where each λ_t can be either 1 or 2. Also suppose that the information structure is given by the history of the state process and that the price of some good for delivery at date 2 contingent on state ω is given by

$$\tilde{q}_2(\omega) = \lambda_1 + \lambda_2.$$

Finally, let A_{ij} be the event that $\lambda_1 = i$ and $\lambda_2 = j$, and suppose

$$P(A_{ij}) = \begin{cases} 1/8 & \text{if } i \neq j \\ 3/8 & \text{if } i = j. \end{cases}$$

What is the price of one unit of the good delivered at date 2 in event A, where A is the event that $\lambda_2 = 1$?

Problems 3.4 through 3.11 pertain to the one-sector model without uncertainty.

3.4. Prove that, at any solution of the Pareto problem, the consumer will sell his entire holdings of capital at each period, that is, $-x_{2t} = z_t$.

3.5. Verify Assumption 3.2.

3.6. Use the concavity of f to verify Assumption 3.4.

3.7. Show that the production plan y defined in connection with the verification of Assumption 3.5 above is an interior point of Y, that is, show that for $\varepsilon > 0$ but sufficiently small, if $y' \in L$ is such that $\|y' - y\|_\infty < \varepsilon$, then $y' \in Y$. Also show that there are no saturation points in X since u is strictly monotone increasing.

3.8. Show that it is possible to choose $\varepsilon > 0$ such that
$$\varepsilon \leqslant \min\{k', Q/8\}$$
and
$$3F(k')/4 + k'/4 + 2\varepsilon \leqslant F(k' - \varepsilon),$$
where $Q = f(k') - \delta k$ and $k' = \min(\hat{k}, \bar{k})/2$.

3.9. Show that if x is such that $\|x - x^0\|_\infty < \varepsilon$, then $x \in X \cap Y$, where x^0 is defined following condition (3.15), and ε is chosen as in Exercise 3.8.

3.10. Show that, if $p_{it} < 0$ for all i and t, then $px^* < 0$.

3.11. Prove that the value of the equilibrium allocation $x^* = y^*$ at the equilibrium prices is
$$px^* = \sum_{t=1}^{\infty} p_{1t} c_t^* - p_{21} \bar{k}.$$

3.12. Suppose that the consumer now has one unit of time per period which he may allocate in any way between labor and leisure in each period. Assume his one period utility function is $u(c,n) = \ell n c + \ell n(1 - n)$, where c is consumption and n is labor supplied in that period. Also assume that the firm's output is $F(k,n) = Ak^\alpha n^{1-\alpha}$, where n is labor input, k is capital input, and $0 < \alpha < 1$. This output may be divided in any way between consumption goods and capital for next period.

Define the consumption and production possibility sets X and Y for this environment and set up the Pareto problem. Compute the competitive equilibrium paths of prices and quantities and especially characterize the rest point.

3.13. Suppose we introduce a new commodity in each period called "bonds." A bond is a consol that promises to pay one unit of the consumption good in each period forever, starting in the period *after* it is purchased. Consumers may purchase and sell bonds but may not issue them. Firms may purchase, sell, and issue bonds. Moreover, suppose *only firms* may hold capital. Also assume that firms must pay taxes at rate θ on their "real net taxable income." This latter term is defined to be total output net of actual physical depreciation and interest payments. Assume that consumers must pay taxes at rate τ on their real purchases of consumption goods plus their interest income. (Assume that the proceeds of these taxes simply vanish from the environment each period.) You may assume that $\bar{k} \geqslant k^*$, where $k^* \in (0,\hat{k})$ is a rest point for problem (P).

Using the one-sector model under certainty as the basic environment, characterize the steady-state prices and quantities of this economy. (*Hint*: Setting up the commodity space, the sets X and Y and consumer preferences are tricky and crucial. Remember that if taxable income is negative, taxes are zero.)

Problems 3.14 through 3.21 pertain to the one-sector model with uncertainty.

3.14. Show that the Pareto problem is Problem $(\tilde{P})$ previously discussed.

3.15. Verify Assumptions 3.1, 3.2, and 3.4.

3.16. Show that y defined by (3.49) and (3.50) is an element of Y and there exists $k' > \varepsilon > 0$ such that (3.51) and (3.52) hold. Verify that the nonnegativity and nonpositivity constraints of Y hold for any y' such that $\|y' - y\| < \varepsilon$.

3.17. Show that the consumption possibility set contains no saturation points.

3.18. Verify Assumptions 3.6 and 3.7.

3.19. Suppose $F(k,r) = A(r)k^r$ for $0 < a \leqslant r \leqslant b < 1$, where $A(r)$ is a positive function of r. Let $\bar{r} = E(r)$, $\bar{A} = E(\ln A(r))$ and assume $u(c) = \ln c$. Show that $v^*(k,r) = K_1 + K_2 \ln F(k,r)$ solves (3.37) and find the correct values of K_1 and K_2 in terms of β, $\bar{r}$, $\bar{A}$. Show that the optimal policy is $g(k,r) = (1 - \beta\bar{r})F(k,r)$.

3.20. In Exercise 3.19 assume that $\bar{r} = 1/2$ with probability $1/3$ and $\bar{r} = 1/3$ with probability $2/3$. Also let $A(1/2) = 24$, $A(1/3) = 48$, and $\beta = 6/7$. Note that A is not increasing. Show that the steady-state distribution of k is degenerate on $k = 2^6$. (*Hint*: Use Theorem 3.6.)

3.21. Now assume $F(k,r) = rk^{1/2}$, and $\bar{r}$ has probability one-half of being either $2/\beta$ or $4/\beta$. In this case, the distribution of k_{t+1} given k_t is $k_t^{1/2}$ with probability $1/2$ and $2k_t^{1/2}$ with probability $1/2$. The distribution of k_t given $k_0 = 1$ is

$$P(k_t = k \mid k_0 = 1) = \begin{cases} 2^{-t} & \text{if } k \in H_t, \\ 0 & \text{otherwise,} \end{cases}$$

where

$$H_t = \{h \mid h = 2^{i/2^{t-1}} \text{ or } h = 2^{(i/2^{t-1})+1} \text{ for } i = 0, \dots, 2^{t-1} - 1\}.$$

As t approaches infinity, the set H_t approaches $\{2^x \mid x \in [0,2]\}$ and the probabilities of the various exponents, x, are always equal to 2^{-t} for each t.

Therefore, it is reasonable to conjecture that the steady-state $\bar{k}$ is given by

$$\bar{k} = 2^{\bar{x}},$$

where $\bar{x}$ is uniformly distributed on $[0,2]$. Prove this conjecture. Note that by Theorem 3.6, this distribution does not depend on the assumption that $k_0 = 1$.

NOTES

1. Most of the material in the first section of this chapter is based on Debreu (1954). The second section is based on Prescott–Lucas (1972). See also Bewley (1972).
2. A binary relation R on a set A is called a *preorder* if it is reflexive and transitive, that is, if (1) for each $a \in A$, $a\,R\,a$, and (2) if, for a, b, and c in A, if $a\,R\,b$ and $b\,R\,c$, then $a\,R\,c$. A preorder is *complete* if any two elements are comparable, that is, if for any a and b in A, either $a\,R\,b$, $b\,R\,a$, or both.
3. Apologies to Al Capp.
4. When we say that U_i "represents" i's preferences, we mean that, for x and x' in X_i, $x' \geqslant_i x$ if and only if $U_i(x') \geqslant U_i(x)$.
5. An alternative way of modeling this economy is to let x_{2t} represent leisure consumed and introduce a third good in each period, x_{3t}, representing labor supplied. This would change the commodity space, the consumption possibility and production possibility sets and the vector ζ as follows:

$$L = \{\{(x_{1t}, x_{2t}, x_{3t})\} \mid \|\{x_{it}\}\|_\infty < \infty, \quad i = 1, 2, 3\},$$
$$X_i = \{x \in L \mid x_{1t} \geqslant 0,\ x_{2t} \geqslant 0,\ x_{3t} \leqslant 0,\ x_{2t} - x_{3t} \leqslant 1,\ t = 1, 2, \ldots\},$$
$$Y_j = \{y \in L \mid 0 \leqslant y_{1t} \leqslant f_j(y_{3t}),\ y_{2t} = y_{3t},\ t = 1, 2, \ldots)\},$$
$$\zeta = \{(\zeta_{1t},\ \zeta_{2t},\ \zeta_{3t})\},$$

where $\zeta_{1t} = \zeta_{3t} = 0$ and $\zeta_{2t} = m$ for all t. The attainability condition now becomes

$$\sum_{i=1}^{m} x_{i1t} - \sum_{j=1}^{n} y_{j1t} = 0, \tag{a}$$

$$\sum_{i=1}^{m} x_{i2t} - \sum_{j=1}^{n} y_{j2t} = m, \tag{b}$$

$$\sum_{i=1}^{m} x_{i3t} - \sum_{i=1}^{n} y_{j3t} = 0, \tag{c}$$

for all t. Note that (b), (c), and the constraint that $y_{j2t} = y_{j3t}$ imply

$$\sum_{i=1}^{m} (x_{i2t} - x_{i3t}) = m,$$

that is, the total labor supplied and the total leisure consumed must add up to the endowment at each date. Since $x_i \in X_i$, so that $x_{i2t} - x_{i3t} \leq 1$ for each i and t, attainability implies that *each* consumer supply any time he does not consume.

Using the fact, previously derived, that, for any attainable allocation, $x_{i3t} = x_{i2t} - 1$, the budget constraint for this formulation can be written

$$\sum_{t=1}^{\infty} [p_{1t}x_{i1t} + (p_{2t} + p_{3t})x_{i2t}] \leq \sum_{t=1}^{\infty} p_{3t}.$$

Note that, if prices are nonnegative and if the endowment of a consumer is to satisfy the budget constraint, it must be the case that $p_{2t} = 0$ for all t. That is, the cost of leisure is simply the opportunity cost of the income foregone by not working, p_{3t}. The right-hand side of the constraint is consumer i's wealth, that is, the present value of his endowment of time

6. While free disposal generally suffices to guarantee that Y has nonempty interior in the sup-norm topology, it does not under other norms. Indeed, the nonnegative orthant of ℓ_2 has empty interior (recall that the norm in ℓ_2 is the square root of the sum of squares of the components). To see this, suppose $\varepsilon > 0$ is given and x is any arbitrary element of the nonnegative orthant of ℓ_2. We will exhibit a point $z \in \ell_2$ which is not in the nonnegative orthant but is within ε of x. Since $\|x\|_2 < \infty$, there exists an N such that for all $n \geq N$, $x_n < \varepsilon/2$. Define $z \in \ell_2$ by $z_n = x_n$ for $n \neq N$, and $z_N = x_N - \varepsilon/2$. Then $z_N < 0$, so z is not in the nonnegative orthant of ℓ_2 but is in ℓ_2. Moreover $\|x - z\|_2 = [(x_N - z_N)^2]^{1/2} = \varepsilon/2 < \varepsilon$. Since ε and x were arbitrary, this shows that the nonnegative orthant of ℓ_2 has empty interior. In general, nonempty interior for infinite dimensional production possibility sets is a very strong assumption. [I am indebted to David Levine for pointing out this fact to me.]

7. An example of an equilibrium with no price representation is as follows. Let the commodity space be $L = \ell_\infty$. There is only one consumer whose consumption possibility set is the nonnegative orthant of L. There is one firm whose production possibility set is

$$Y = \{y \in L \mid 0 \leq y_t \leq 1 + b^t \quad \text{for} \quad t = 1, 2, \ldots\},$$

where $b \in (0,1)$. To define preferences, let S be the subspace of L defined by

$$S = \left\{ x \in \ell_\infty \mid \lim_{N \to \infty} \frac{1}{N} \sum_{t=1}^{N} x_t < \infty \right\}.$$

It is easy to check that S is a linear space, that is, a subspace of L. Define v on S by

$$v(x) = \lim_{N \to \infty} \frac{1}{N} \sum_{t=1}^{N} x_t \quad \text{for} \quad x \in S.$$

It is easy to check that v is a continuous linear form on S and that

$$|v(x)| \leq \|x\|_\infty$$

for every $x \in X$. Thus by the Hahn–Banach extension theorem [Luenberger (1969, p. 111)] v can be extended to a continuous linear form on L (the required sublinear functional is the sup-norm) that agrees with v on S. Denote this extension by U and assume that preferences of the single consumer are defined by U. It is easy to check that this economy satisfies Assumptions (3.1)–(3.5). Now, one Pareto optimum for this economy is $x_t^0 = y_t^0 = 1 + b^t$ for all t. By Theorem 3.2, there is a nontrivial linear form w such that (3.3) and (3.4) hold for $[x^0, y^0, w]$. Suppose w is represented by p. It can be shown that $p_t \geq 0$ for all t, $p_t > 0$ for at least one t, and

$$\sum_{t=1}^{\infty} p_t < \infty.$$

Therefore, if z is the unit vector in L,

$$w(z) = \sum_{t=1}^{\infty} p_t < \sum_{t=1}^{\infty} p_t(1 + b^t) = w(x^0).$$

But

$$U(x^0) = 1 = U(z),$$

which contradicts (3.3).

8. The reason we must introduce the new linear form P is that, in general $v(z^n)$ may not converge to $v(z)$. The following example is due to Lars Hansen. Define the linear form v exactly as in the previous endnote, that is, v is the extension to ℓ_∞ of the average function defined on the subspace on which the average converges. As in the previous endnote, let z be the unit vector so that $z^n = (1, \ldots, 1, 0, 0, \ldots)$, where the first n terms are ones. For this z, $v(z^n) = 0$ for all n while $v(z) = 1$. Note that v cannot be represented as a price sequence in ℓ_1. To see this, suppose that $p = \{p_t\}$ were a representation of v in ℓ_1. Let $z_{(t)} = (0, 0, \ldots, 0, 1, 0, \ldots)$, where the 1 is in the tth place. Then, for any t,

$$\langle p, z_{(t)} \rangle = p_t,$$

where $\langle \ \rangle$ denotes inner product. But $v(z_{(t)}) = 0$. So we see that $p_t = 0$ for all t, that is, p is trivial. Clearly v is not trivial so p cannot represent v. (This exemplifies the well-known fact that the dual of ℓ_1 is ℓ_∞ while the dual of ℓ_∞ *contains* ℓ_1, but is not equal to ℓ_1.)

9. The notation $\|x\|_\infty$ when x_t is a vector in $\mathbf{R}^n$ means

$$\sup\{|x_{it}| \,|\, i = 1, \ldots, n; t = 1, 2, \ldots\}.$$

REFERENCES

Bewley, T., "Existence of Equilibria in Economies with Infinitely Many Commodities," *Journal of Economic Theory*, **4**, 3 (June 1972), pp. 514–540.

Brock, W. A. and L. J. Mirman, "Optimal Economic Growth and Uncertainty: The Discounted Case," *Journal of Economic Theory*, **4**, 3 (June 1972), pp. 479–513.

Debreu, G., "Valuation Equilibrium and Pareto Optimum," *Proceedings of the National Academy of Science*, **XL** (1954), pp. 588–592.

Luenberger, D. G., *Optimization by Vector Space Methods* (New York: Wiley, 1969).

Mirman, L. J., "The Steady State Behavior of A Class of One Sector Growth Models with Uncertain Technology," *Journal of Economic Theory,* **6,** 3 (June 1973), pp. 219–242.

——— "One Sector Economic Growth and Uncertainty: A Survey," in *Stochastic Programming,* M. A. H. Dempster (ed.) (New York: Academic Press, 1980).

Mirman, L. J. and I. Zilcha, "On Optimal Growth Under Uncertainty," *Journal of Economic Theory,* **11** (1975), pp. 329–339.

Prescott, E. C. and R. E. Lucas, Jr., "A Note on Price Systems in Infinite Dimensional Space," *International Economic Review,* **13,** 2 (June 1972), pp. 416–422.

CHAPTER 4

Recursive Competitive Equilibrium

In this chapter, we examine a competitive equilibrium concept that differs from valuation equilibrium in that trading is assumed to occur in every period. The idea is to exploit "recursiveness" or "path independence properties" of a model using dynamic programming techniques as developed in Chapter 2. This will lead to pricing functions and agent's decision rules that depend on a finite (generally small) number of "state variables." Such functions, being time and path independent, lend themselves to time-series estimation procedures.

We start by setting out the general model, following Prescott and Mehra (1980). We then present an application to modeling the prices of securities and an example of one problem with the concept of recursive competitive equilibrium.

4.1 GENERAL MODEL

The economy consists of a continuum of identical, infinitely lived consumers, a finite number of constant-returns-to-scale industries, and a finite number of physical consumption and capital goods. Trading is assumed to take place as follows. At the beginning of a period, individuals sell labor services and stocks of capital to firms. These are used by the firms to produce various capital and consumption goods that are then sold back to the individuals. The latter consume the consumption goods and take the capital into the next period.

The economy is subject to random shocks both to production technologies and to preferences. The vector of shocks realized in period t is denoted $\lambda_t \in \mathbf{R}^n$. The process $\{\lambda_t\}$ is assumed to be a stationary, first-order Markov process with bounded ergodic set Λ (i.e., if $\lambda_t \in \Lambda$, then $\lambda_{t+1} \in \Lambda$

with probability one). The transition probabilities are given by the cumulative distribution function $F: \Lambda \times \Lambda \to [0,1]$, where $F(\lambda', \lambda) = \Pr(\lambda_{t+1} \le \lambda' \mid \lambda_t = \lambda)$.

There are assumed to be m_1 physical consumption goods and m_2 physical capital goods available in the economy. A *period commodity bundle* is a vector

$$x = (x_1, x_2, x_3) \in \mathbf{R}_+^{m_1} \times \mathbf{R}_-^{m_2} \times \mathbf{R}_+^{m_2} = \hat{\mathbf{R}}^m,$$

where $m = m_1 + 2m_2$, x_1 is a vector of consumption goods consumed or produced in the period, x_2 is a vector of capital goods sold to firms or bought by firms in the period, and x_3 is a vector of capital goods bought by or sold to consumers at the end of the period. Using the same sign convention as in Chapter 3, x_2 will be nonpositive.

Each individual faces two sets of constraints on the period commodity bundles he may choose in any period. The first set reflects general constraints that do not depend on past decisions such as the constraints that labor supplied may not exceed available time. These constraints are modeled by requiring that $x \in X \subset \hat{\mathbf{R}}^m$. In addition, each consumer is constrained not to sell more capital in each period than he has available at the beginning of the period. This is modeled using the *period consumption possibility set* given $k \in \mathbf{R}_+^{m_2}$,

$$X(k) = \{x \in X \mid -k \le x_2 \le 0\}$$

by requiring, for each t, that $x_{t+1} \in X(x_{3t})$. In addition to X and $X(k)$, the consumer is described by a *period utility function* $u: X \times \Lambda \to \mathbf{R}$, and a discount factor $\beta \in (0,1)$. The function u and the factor β determine the consumer's preferences over sequences of random period commodity bundles x_t, where $x_t: \Omega \to X$, $\Omega = \Lambda \times \Lambda \times \cdots$, and x_t is Φ_t-measurable, where $\{\Phi_t\}$ is the filtration determined by the history of the $\{\lambda_t\}$ process. Their preferences are defined by

$$E\left\{\sum_{t=1}^{\infty} \beta^{t-1} u(x_{1t}, \lambda_t)\right\},$$

where the expectation is taken over all realizations of the random process $\{\lambda_t\}$ using the measure induced by the Markov transition function F.

The set X, the correspondence $X(k)$, the function u and the number β are assumed to be the same for all consumers. Also each is assumed to start with the same vector of capital stocks at date 1. There is a measure space of consumers, namely $(I, B(I), \mu)$, where $B(I)$ is the set of Borel subsets of the unit interval I and μ is Lebesgue measure.

Each firm in a given industry produces under the same technology as all other firms in the industry. For industry j $(j = 1, \ldots, J)$ this technology is given by a correspondence $Y_j(\lambda) \subset \hat{\mathbf{R}}^m$, that is, given the current shock λ, any firm in industry j may choose any period commodity bundle in $Y_j(\lambda)$

for that period. Given λ, $Y_j(\lambda)$ is called the *period production possibility set* for industry j. Note that feasible period production bundles for a given period are not related to past decisions of the firm. We denote by $Y(\lambda)$ the aggregate period production possibility set

$$Y(\lambda) = \sum_{j=1}^{J} Y_j(\lambda).$$

The following assumptions are maintained.

Assumption 4.1 F is continuous in both arguments.

Assumption 4.2 X is closed and convex.

Assumption 4.3 u is continuous in both arguments, strictly increasing, strictly concave, and differentiable in x_1.

Assumption 4.4 For any j, λ, $Y_j(\lambda)$ is a closed, convex cone, that is, if $y \in Y_j(\lambda)$ and $\gamma \geqslant 0$, then $\gamma y \in Y_j(\lambda)$.

Assumption 4.5 There exists a bounded set K contained in $\mathbf{R}_+^{m_2}$ such that if $k \in K$, $\lambda \in \Lambda$, and $y \in X(k) \cap Y(\lambda)$, then $y_3 \in K$. Also, $X(k) \cap Y(\lambda)$ is continuous as a correspondence in (k, λ).

Assumptions 4.1–4.3 are straightforward. Assumption 4.4 is the constant-returns-to-scale assumption on the period production possibility sets of firms. Although this may seem like a strong assumption, in fact, it is not. Given a decreasing-returns-to-scale technology, one can convert this into a constant-returns-to-scale technology by adding another factor of production. For example, suppose $g : \mathbf{R}_+^n \to \mathbf{R}_+$ is a strictly concave production function. Denoting inputs by x and output by y, $\{(x,y) \in \mathbf{R}_+^n \times \mathbf{R}_+ \mid y \leqslant g(x)\}$ is a convex production possibility set, but not a convex cone. If we add the factor z and define a new production technology $G : \mathbf{R}_+^{n+1} \to \mathbf{R}_+$ by $G(x,z) = zg(x/z)$ if $z \neq 0$ and $G(x,0) \equiv 0$, then G is homogeneous of degree 1, $G(x,1) = g(x)$, and $\{(x,z,y) \in \mathbf{R}_+^{n+1} \times \mathbf{R} \mid y \leqslant G(x,z)\}$ is a convex cone. Thus the decreasing returns technology g is equivalent to the constant returns technology G along with the restriction $z = 1$, which can be incorporated in X. This is nothing more than a formalization of the old idea that if *all* factors of production could be increased in proportion, then output would increase in the same proportion. In this view diminishing returns to scale comes about because at least one factor—for example, the size of the earth—cannot be increased in proportion with the others.

Assumption 4.5 guarantees that the economy is not capable of producing an infinite amount of output. This will be satisfied if, for example, some factor like labor is essential for production and its supply is bounded. The continuity of $X(\cdot) \cap Y(\cdot)$ assures existence of Pareto optima and continuity of the value of a Pareto optimal plan as a function of the state variables.

The relevant state variables for an individual in this economy are his own current stocks of capital goods, k, the capital stocks of other consumers, and the current realization λ of the stochastic shock. Since all other consumers are the same, a representative consumer can assume that they all have the same capital stocks, $\underline{k}$ (although he believes he is free to choose his own k independent of their choices). Thus the state of an individual is summarized by $(k, \underline{k}, \lambda) \in K \times K \times \Lambda$. The state of the economy is just $(\underline{k}, \lambda)$.

Consumers are viewed as choosing a policy $x : K \times K \times \Lambda \to X$ giving the period commodity bundle as a function of their current state so as to maximize the preferences described above subject to $x(k, \underline{k}, \lambda) \in X(k)$ and a budget constraint. This budget constraint is determined by a vector of prices $p = (p_1, \ldots, p_m)$ of the commodities the consumers take to be given functions of the state of the economy $(\underline{k}, \lambda)$, that is, $p : K \times \Lambda \to \hat{\mathbf{R}}^m$. The pricing function p describes how prices will evolve given the evolution of the state. While the evolution of k is determined by the consumer's purchases of capital at the end of the period, that is, $k' = x_3$, and λ evolves according to $F(\lambda', \lambda)$, the consumer must view the evolution of other consumers' capital stocks as exogenous. Suppose we denote by $f(\underline{k}, \lambda)$ the capital stocks $\underline{k}'$ of all other consumers next period given their current stocks $\underline{k}$ and the current shock λ. Later, the functions p and f will be determined in equilibrium.

Given a pricing function p and an equation of motion f for $\underline{k}$, the representative consumer's infinite horizon maximization problem can be formulated as a stationary discounted dynamic programming problem as in Chapter 2. Here

$$S = K \times K \times \Lambda,$$
$$D(s) = D(k, \underline{k}, \lambda) = \{x \in X(k) \mid p(\underline{k}, \lambda)x \leqslant 0\},$$
$$dq(s' \mid s, x) = \begin{cases} 0 & \text{if } k' \neq x_3 \text{ or } k' \neq f(\underline{k}, \lambda) \\ dF(\lambda', \lambda) & \text{otherwise,} \end{cases}$$

where $s = (k, \underline{k}, \lambda)$, $s' = (k', \underline{k}', \lambda')$,

$$r(s, x) = u(x_1, \lambda).$$

The optimality equation for this problem is

$$v(k, \underline{k}, \lambda) = \max_{x \in X(k)} u(x_1, \lambda) + \beta \int v(x_3, f(\underline{k}, \lambda), \lambda') \, dF(\lambda', \lambda) \qquad (4.1)$$

subject to $p(\underline{k}, \lambda)x \leqslant 0$.

Firms are viewed as choosing a policy $y: K \times \Lambda \rightarrow \hat{\mathbf{R}}^m$ giving the period production plan as a function of the current state of the economy so as to maximize profits at current prices $p(\underline{k}, \lambda)$ subject to the technology constraint $y \in Y_j(\lambda)$. Note that since firms can sell their capital at the end of any period (y_3) in a competitive market, the firm's profit maximization problem is static.[1] Also, with constant returns to scale, firm profits will be zero in equilibrium, so we needn't worry about who owns the firm.

We may now define equilibrium as follows.

Definition 4.1 A *Recursive Competitive Equilibrium* (RCE) is

1. an almost everywhere continuous pricing function $p^*: K \times \Lambda \rightarrow \hat{\mathbf{R}}^m$,
2. an almost everywhere continuous value function $v^*: K \times K \times \Lambda \rightarrow \mathbf{R}$,
3. a consumer's policy $x^*: K \times K \times \Lambda \rightarrow X$,
4. a J-tuplet of period production plans $y_j^*: K \times \Lambda \rightarrow \hat{\mathbf{R}}^m$, $j = 1, \ldots, J$, and
5. a continuous law of motion $f^*: K \times \Lambda \rightarrow K$

such that for all $(k, \underline{k}, \lambda) \in K \times K \times \Lambda$:

i. v^* solves the optimality equation (4.1), x^* attains v^* given $p \equiv p^*$ and $f \equiv f^*$,
ii. for each $j = 1, \ldots, J$, $y_j^*(\underline{k}, \lambda)$ solves

$$\max_{y \in Y_j(\lambda)} p^*(\underline{k}, \lambda) y,$$

iii.

$$\sum_{j=1}^{J} y_j^*(\underline{k}, \lambda) = \int_I x^*(\underline{k}, \underline{k}, \lambda) \, d\mu = x^*(\underline{k}, \underline{k}, \lambda), \quad \text{and}$$

iv.

$$f^*(\underline{k}, \lambda) = x_3^*(\underline{k}, \underline{k}, \lambda).$$

Conditions (i) and (ii) are self-explanatory. Condition (iii) is simply that supply equals demand (given $k = \underline{k}$) at the equilibrium prices p^*. Condition (iv) says that the representative consumer's optimal choice of capital stock for next period is the same as the choices he assumed all other consumers would make given that everyone starts with the same stocks, that is, $k = \underline{k}$.

The "equal weight" Pareto optimal allocation of the model is found by chosing sequences $\{x_t\}$ and $\{k_t\}$ to solve

$$\max E\left\{ \sum_{t=1}^{\infty} \beta^{t-1} u(x_{1t}, \lambda_t) \mid k_1, \lambda_1 \right\}$$

subject to

$$x_t \in X(k_t) \cap Y(\lambda_t),$$
$$k_{t+1} = x_{3t} \quad \text{for all} \quad t,$$
$$k_1, \lambda_1 \quad \text{given.}$$

This problem can also be formulated as a dynamic programming problem with $S = K \times \Lambda$, $D(k,\lambda) = X(k) \cap Y(\lambda)$,

$$dq(k',\lambda' \mid k,\lambda,x) = \begin{cases} 0 & \text{if } k' \neq x_3 \\ dF(\lambda',\lambda) & \text{otherwise,} \end{cases}$$

and $r(k,\lambda,x) = u(x_1,\lambda)$. The optimality equation is

$$w(k,\lambda) = \max_{x \in X(k) \cap Y(\lambda)} u(x_1,\lambda) + \beta \int w(x_3,\lambda') \, dF(\lambda',\lambda). \tag{4.2}$$

It can be shown that a unique, continuous, bounded solution w^* of (4.2) and an optimal policy $\delta^*(k,\lambda)$ exist (see Exercise 4.1). Moreover, using Assumption 4.6 discussed later, it can be shown that w^* is concave and strictly increasing in k (see Exercise 4.2). Being concave and continuous in k, w^* is differentiable with respect to k almost everywhere.

The main results are the two theorems of welfare economics.

Theorem 4.1   Under Assumptions 4.1–4.5, every RCE is a Pareto optimum.

Proof   See Prescott–Mehra (1980), p. 1373.

The converse requires one more assumption.

Assumption 4.6   If $k_A > k_B$ (strict inequality for at least one component), then for any λ and $x_B \in X(k_B) \cap Y(\lambda)$ there exists $x_A \in X(k_A) \cap Y(\lambda)$ such that $x_A > x_B$ and $x_{1A} > x_{1B}$.

The assumption implies that with more capital, more current consumption of some good is possible without any reduction in current consumption of any other goods or in next period's capital stocks.

Theorem 4.2   Under Assumptions 4.1–4.6, if δ^* is any Pareto optimal policy attaining w^*, then there exists an RCE, v^*, p^*, f^*, x^*, y^* in which

$$v^*(\underline{k},\underline{k},\lambda) \equiv w^*(\underline{k},\lambda), \quad x^*(\underline{k},\underline{k},\lambda) \equiv \delta^*(\underline{k},\lambda) \equiv y^*(\underline{k},\lambda), \quad \text{and} \quad f^* \equiv \delta_3^*.$$

Proof   See Prescott–Mehra (1980), p. 1373.

Note that since a Pareto optimum exists, so does an RCE. If the former is unique, so is the latter. Also since an RCE is Pareto optimal, its allocation is also the allocation of a valuation equilibrium (when one exists). The RCE prices are relative prices *within a given period* and thus are not the same as the prices associated with a valuation equilibrium, although generally there will be a relationship between them. Bewley (1980) describes this relationship for the asset pricing model of Lucas (1978), which is presented in the next section [see also Prescott–Mehra (1980)].

4.2 APPLICATION AND ADDITIONAL COMMENT

Perhaps one of the most important applications of the RCE concept is to models of security prices that involve explicit dynamics. One elegant example of such an "Intertemporal Capital Asset Pricing Model" or ICAPM is Lucas (1978) previously mentioned.

Lucas models essentially a pure exchange economy with one physical good, $m_1 = 1$. Firms are able to supply output of the single good at zero cost up to an exogenously specified capacity constraint that fluctuates over time. Firm j's capacity constraint at date t is denoted λ_{jt}. The nonnegative vector process $\{\lambda_t\}$, where $\lambda_t = (\lambda_{1t}, \ldots, \lambda_{nt})$, is assumed to be first-order Markov with continuous transition function

$$F(\lambda', \lambda) = \Pr[\lambda_{t+1} \leq \lambda' \mid \lambda_t = \lambda].$$

Following Prescott and Mehra, we model capital in this economy as the right to use the production technology just described. That is, there are $m_2 = n$ capital goods (so that $m = 2n + 1$), where one unit of capital good j in period t is interpreted as the right to produce up to λ_{jt} units of output for free in that period (x_{2j} units of capital good j is the right to produce up to $-x_{2j}\lambda_{jt}$ units). Note that owning the right to produce is like owning the firm, and that owning part of such a right is like owning that part of the equity of an all-equity financed firm. Consequently, we will henceforth refer to these rights as "shares." In this terminology then, each firm is all-equity financed and has one share outstanding. We are interested in the equilibrium prices of these shares.

The firm is not allowed to produce the capital good. Thus the production possibility set of firm j is

$$Y_j(\lambda) = \{y \in \hat{\mathbf{R}}^m \mid y_1 \leq -y_{2j}\lambda_j, \ y_3 \leq -y_2\}.$$

Obviously, in equilibrium, firm j will not purchase capital good i for $i \neq j$.

There is one representative consumer whose preferences are not state dependent:

$$U(x) = E \sum_{t=1}^{\infty} \beta^{t-1} u(x_{1t}),$$

where u satisfies assumption 4.3. The period consumption possibility set of the consumer, if he starts the period with $k = (k_1, \ldots, k_n)$ units of the n capital goods, is given by

$$X(k) = \{x \in \hat{\mathbf{R}}^m \mid x_2 \geqslant -k\}.$$

The initial value of k is simply $e = (1, \ldots, 1)$.

Obviously the unique Pareto optimal allocation for this economy involves

$$x_{1t} = \sum_{j=1}^{n} \lambda_{jt}, \quad y_{1jt} = \lambda_{jt} \quad \text{for all } j \text{ and } t,$$

$$x_{2jt} = y_{2jjt} = -1, \quad x_{3jt} = y_{3jjt} = 1 \quad \text{for all } j \text{ and } t,$$

$$y_{2ijt} = y_{3ijt} = 0 \quad \text{for} \quad i \neq j \quad \text{and} \quad t,$$

where $-y_{2ijt}$ is the amount of firm i's capacity purchased by firm j at the beginning of period t, and y_{3ijt} is the amount of firm i's capacity sold by firm j at the end of period t. That is, consumers supply all their capital each period, firm j buys only type j capital and produces all the output it can each period, then sells its capital back to the consumer.

Since it is easy to check that Assumptions 4.1–4.6 are satisfied (see Exercise 4.3), an RCE exists. Let $[p^*, v^*, x^*, (y_j^*), f^*]$ be the RCE that supports the Pareto optimal allocation. Thus $f^*(k, \lambda) \equiv k$.

First consider the profit maximization problem of firm j using prices p^*,

$$\max\{p^* y \mid y \in Y_j(\lambda)\}.$$

If y^* solves this problem, it can be shown (see Exercise 4.4) that $p_1^* > 0$ and $p_{2j}^* = p_{3j}^* + \lambda_j$. Thus the value of owning a share in firm j at the beginning of any period is simply the output of firm j in that period, that is, the current dividend, plus the value of the share as of the end of the period. Since the firms' and consumer's problems are all homogeneous of degree zero in p^* and $p_1^* > 0$, we may assume $p_1^* \equiv 1$ without loss of generality.

Next consider the consumer's utility maximization problem (4.1), with $p = p^*$ and $f = f^*$. We know, by choice of RCE, that v^* is the value function for this problem. It is clear that, in any solution, $x_2 = -k$. Consequently, we may impose the constraint $x_2 = -k$ without loss of generality. Using the above results, we can restate the consumer's problem with $p = p^*$ and $f = f^*$ as

$$v^*(k, \underline{k}, \lambda) = \max_{c, z} u(c) + \beta E[v^*(z, \underline{k}, \lambda') \mid \lambda]$$

subject to

$$c \geqslant 0, \quad z \geqslant 0, \quad \text{and} \quad c + p_3^* z \leqslant p_2^* k,$$

where the expectation is taken with respect to F. It can be shown, as in Exercises 4.1 and 4.2, that v^* is concave and strictly increasing in its first argument and a unique optimal policy $[c^*(k,\underline{k},\lambda), z^*(k,\underline{k},\lambda)]$ exists. We wish to calculate the derivative of v^* with respect to k at any $(k,\underline{k},\lambda)$ such that $c^*(k,\underline{k},\lambda) > 0$. Let $s^0 = (k^0,\underline{k}^0,\lambda^0)$ be such a state, and consider the suboptimal policy defined by

$$z(s) = \begin{cases} z^*(s^0) & \text{if } p_3^*(\hat{s})z^*(s^0) \leqslant p_2^*(\hat{s})k \\ k & \text{otherwise,} \end{cases}$$

$$c(s) = p_2^*(\hat{s})k - p_3^*(\hat{s})z(s),$$

where $s = (k,\underline{k},\lambda)$ and $\hat{s} = (\underline{k},\lambda)$. It can now be shown, as in the proof of Theorem 2.5, that

$$\frac{\partial v^*(s^0)}{\partial k_j} = u'[c^*(s^0)][\lambda_j^0 + p_{3j}^*(\hat{s}^0)].$$

The first-order conditions for the consumer's problem now imply that

$$p_{3j}^*(\underline{k},\lambda)u'[c^*(k,\underline{k},\lambda)]$$
$$= \beta E\{u'[c^*(z^*(k,\underline{k},\lambda),\underline{k},\lambda')][\lambda_j' + p_{3j}^*(\underline{k},\lambda')] \mid \lambda\} \qquad (4.3)$$

provided $c^*[z^*(k,\underline{k},\lambda),\underline{k},\lambda'] > 0$ for almost every λ'. Equation (4.3) is the basic relationship among asset prices, some form of which appears in all ICAPM models. It can be interpreted as follows. The cost today of buying marginally more of a share in a firm j (for tomorrow) is p_{3j}^* units of consumption, or, in utility terms, the expression on the left-hand side of (4.3). This extra fraction of a share can be sold for

$$p_{2j}^*(\underline{k},\lambda') = p_{3j}^*(\underline{k},\lambda') + \lambda_j'$$

units of the consumption good tomorrow if tomorrow's state is λ'. Therefore, the right-hand side of (4.3) represents the expected benefit of buying marginally more of a share in firm j today, so Equation (4.3) simply says that the costs and benefits of additional shares in any firm are equated at the margin.

Since we know that, for our Pareto optimal solution, $k = \underline{k} = e$ and $c^*(e,e,\lambda) = \lambda e$, (4.3) can be written as

$$u'(\lambda e)p_{3j}^*(e,\lambda) = \beta E\{u'(\lambda' e)[\lambda_j' + p_{3j}^*(e,\lambda')] \mid \lambda\}, \qquad (4.4)$$

which is equation (6) in Lucas (1978). Lucas uses (4.4) to characterize p_3^* as follows. First, since we are interested only in p_3^* evaluated at (e,λ), we will henceforth abbreviate $p_{3j}^*(e,\lambda)$ to simply $p_j(\lambda)$. Now write (4.4) as

$$u'(\lambda e)p_j(\lambda) = g_j(\lambda) + \beta E\{u'(\lambda' e)p_j(\lambda') \mid \lambda\}, \qquad (4.5)$$

where

$$g_j(\lambda) = \beta E\{u'(\lambda' e)\lambda_j' \mid \lambda\}.$$

Now suppose f_j solves the functional equation

$$f(\lambda) = g_j(\lambda) + \beta E\{f(\lambda') \mid \lambda\}. \qquad (4.6)$$

Then, comparing (4.5) and (4.6), we see that

$$f_j(\lambda) = u'(\lambda e)p_j(\lambda)$$

or

$$p_j(\lambda) = f_j(\lambda)/u'(\lambda e).$$

To solve (4.6), let T_j be the operator defined by the right-hand side of (4.6). It is easy to check that, if $u(0) = 0$, then T_j maps bounded, continuous functions $f : \mathbf{R}_+^n \to \mathbf{R}_+$ into the same set of functions and that T_j is a contraction mapping on that set (see Exercise 4.5). Therefore,

$$f_j = \lim_{n \to \infty} T_j^n f \quad \text{for any bounded, continuous } f : \mathbf{R}_+^n \to \mathbf{R}_+.$$

While it is not possible to derive useful properties for f_j in general, some interesting special cases can be analyzed. One such case is if u is linear (in this case we may take u to be the identity without loss of generality). For linear u, it can be shown that, for any t,

$$f_j(\lambda) = p_j(\lambda) = \sum_{s=1}^{\infty} \beta^s E[\lambda_{j,t+s} \mid \lambda_t = \lambda],$$

that is, the price of a share is simply the discounted sum of the expected future dividends. This relation can also be written

$$p_j(\lambda) = \beta E[\lambda_j' + p_j(\lambda_j') \mid \lambda],$$

which is a Martingale adjusted for dividends and discounting. This Martingale-like property will not hold in general.

The Lucas model is an interesting application of the Recursive Competitive Equilibrium (more accurately, the RCE is a generalization of the Lucas model). It exploits heavily the relationship between a Pareto optimal allocation and the RCE in the representative consumer framework. In general, however, the RCE model lacks many contingent claims provided for in the valuation equilibrium setup. As Bewley (1980) points out, this is likely to cause any RCE to be Pareto suboptimal if there are heterogeneous consumers. The following example will illustrate this point.

Heterogeneous consumer example

The economy consists of one consumption good ($m_1 = 1$), one capital good ($m_2 = 1$), two consumers, one firm, and two dates.[2] The consumption possibility set of consumer i is simply $\mathbf{R}^m$, for $i = 1, 2$. Consumer 1's preferences are given by

$$U_1(x_1) = u(x_{111}) + u(x_{112}),$$

where x_{1it} is consumer i's consumption at date t, $t = 1, 2$, and u is strictly concave and strictly increasing. Consumer 2's preferences are given by

$$U_2(x_2) = x_{121} + x_{122}.$$

Each consumer is endowed with $k_i = 1$ unit of capital, $i = 1, 2$. Note that consumer 1 is strictly risk averse (since u is strictly concave), while consumer 2 is risk neutral. The basic idea in this example is that an optimal allocation involves consumer 2 insuring consumer 1 against risks arising from the fact that the state of nature in the second period is uncertain in the first period. The RCE framework, however, does not allow these two consumers to trade contingent claims to second period consumption, which could be used to effect this insurance.

The firm has a linear production technology for the consumption good and cannot produce the capital good. The firm's production possibility set is given by

$$Y(\lambda) = \{y \in \hat{\mathbf{R}}^m \mid y_1 \leq -\lambda y_2, \, y_3 \leq -y_2\}.$$

The first-period state of nature, λ_1, is known to be 1, however the second-period state, is random. Its distribution is given by

$$\lambda_2 = \begin{cases} 1 & \text{with probability } q, \\ 2 & \text{with probability } 1 - q. \end{cases}$$

The state of the economy, and the state of each individual, in this economy is specified by (k_1, k_2, λ). We will construct an RCE by working backwards from period 2. Given a price system $p(k_1, k_2, \lambda)$ with p_{1t} normalized to unity for $t = 1, 2$, the demand of consumer i is determined by choosing $x \in X_i(k_i)$ to

$$\max u_i(x_{1i2})$$

subject to

$$x_{1i2} + p_{22}(s)x_{2i2} + p_{32}(s)x_{3i2} \leq 0,$$

where $u_1 = u$, u_2 is the identity map, and $s = (k_1, k_2, \lambda_2)$. Assuming that $p_{22} > 0$, then the solution clearly involves $x_{2i2} = -k_i$, and $x_{1i2} = k_i p_{22}(s)$. Therefore, aggregate demand for consumption in period 2, x_{12}, and aggregate supply of capital in period 2, x_{22}, will be given by

$$x_{12} = (k_1 + k_2)p_{22}(s),$$
$$x_{22} = -(k_1 + k_2).$$

Now consider the firm's problem: choose $y \in Y(\lambda_2)$ to

$$\max y_{12} + p_{22}(s)y_{22} + p_{32}(s)y_{32}.$$

Since the world ends after period 2, it is reasonable to conjecture that capital delivered at the end of period 2 will be worthless in equilibrium, that is, that $p_{32} \equiv 0$. In this case, the firm will be indifferent as to how much of the capital it purchased at the beginning of the period to supply at the end. Similarly, the consumer will also be indifferent, and we can choose any amount not in excess of $-y_{22}$ to clear the market. It is convenient to choose $y_{32} = x_{312} = x_{322} = 0$. Since the firm's problem is linear in y_{12}, and its coefficient in the objective function is positive, it is obvious that the optimal output of the consumption good in period 2 is $-\lambda_2 y_{22}$, that is, the firm will produce all the consumption good it can. The firm's problem can now be restated (assuming $p_{32} = 0$) as

$$\max_{y_{22} \le 0} -y_{22}(\lambda_2 - p_{22}).$$

It is now clear that the firm will not choose to purchase a positive, finite amount of capital in period 2 unless $p_{22} = \lambda_2$. Since, in equilibrium, we know that the aggregate supply of capital will be 2, it must be the case that $p_{22} = \lambda_2$. In this case, the firm is indifferent as to how much of the consumption good it produces at period 2. Consequently, we may take $y_{22} = -(k_1 + k_2)$ and $y_{12} = (k_1 + k_2)\lambda_2$.

Now consider the consumers' problems at date 1. Since $x_{1i2} = k_i \lambda_2$, the value function for consumer i at date 2 is

$$v_i(k_1, k_2, \lambda_2) = u_i(k_i \lambda_2).$$

Therefore, consumer i's problem at date 1 is to choose $x \in X_i(1)$ to

$$\max u_i(x_{1i1}) + q u_i(x_{3i1}) + (1 - q)u_i(2x_{3i1})$$

subject to

$$x_{1i1} + p_{21}(1,1,1)x_{2i1} + p_{31}(1,1,1)x_{3i1} \le 0.$$

Assuming that $p_{21} > 0$, it is clear that the solution involves selling one's entire capital stock, that is, $x_{2i1} = -1$. The first-order conditions for an interior solution for the other variables are

$$u_i'(x_{1i1}) = \gamma,$$
$$q u_i'(x_{3i1}) + 2(1 - q)u_i'(2x_{3i1}) = \gamma p_{31},$$

where $\gamma \ge 0$ is a Lagrange multiplier for the budget constraint. For $i = 2$, we have $u_2' \equiv 1$. This implies that $\gamma = 1$ and $p_{31} = 2 - q$.

The solution of the firm's problem at date 1 with $p_{31} > 0$ (as just shown) clearly involves $y_{11} = -\lambda_1 y_{21} = -y_{21}$ and $y_{31} = -y_{21} = y_{11}$. Substituting these values into the profit function results in the problem

$$\max y_{11}(1 - p_{21} + p_{31})$$

over $y_{11} \ge 0$. In order that the firm choose y_{11} equal to the quantity of consumption goods demanded, we must have $1 - p_{21} + p_{31} = 0$, or

$$p_{21} = 1 + p_{31} = 3 - q.$$

To summarize, we have shown that if prices are given by

$$p_{22}(k_1, k_2, \lambda_2) = \lambda_2, \tag{4.7}$$

$$p_{32}(k_1, k_2, \lambda_2) = 0, \tag{4.8}$$

$$p_{21}(1,1,1) = 3 - q, \tag{4.9}$$

$$p_{31}(1,1,1) = 2 - q, \tag{4.10}$$

then:

1. Consumers and the firm are indifferent with regard to capital for delivery at the end of period 2. We may therefore assume that

$$x_{312} = x_{322} = y_{32} = 0. \tag{4.11}$$

2. The firm is indifferent as to how much capital it purchases at the beginning of period 2, but will produce as much consumption output as possible. Consumers demand

$$x_{1i2} = x_{3i1}\lambda_2 \quad \text{for } i = 1, 2, \tag{4.12}$$

units of consumption goods and supply

$$x_{2i2} = -x_{3i1} \quad \text{for } i = 1, 2, \tag{4.13}$$

units of capital goods at the beginning of period 2. Therefore, we may assume that

$$y_{22} = x_{212} + x_{222} = -(x_{311} + x_{321}), \tag{4.14}$$

and, hence

$$y_{12} = x_{112} + x_{122} = (x_{311} + x_{321})\lambda_2. \tag{4.15}$$

3. Consumer i supplies

$$x_{2i1} = -1 \tag{4.16}$$

units of capital in period 1. Consumer 1's demand for consumption goods in period 1 satisfies

$$u'(x_{111}) = 1. \tag{4.17}$$

The firm is indifferent about its output of consumption goods, so we may assume it purchases the two units of capital supplied, that is,

$$y_{21} = -2 = x_{211} + x_{221} \tag{4.18}$$

and produces

$$y_{11} = 2\lambda_1 = 2 \tag{4.19}$$

units of consumption goods in period 1. Consumer 2 is also indifferent among all bundles $(x_{121}, -1, x_{321})$ that satisfy his budget constraint at prices given by (4.7)–(4.10). Therefore, if $u'(2) < 1$, we can assume that consumer 2 chooses

$$x_{121} = 2 - x_{111}, \tag{4.20}$$

so that supply of the consumption good in period 1 equals the demand. Similarly, consumer 1's demand for capital at the end of period 1 satisfies

$$qu'(x_{311}) + 2(1-q)u'(2x_{311}) = 2 - q.$$

The firm's supply of capital at the end of period 1 is

$$y_{31} = -y_{21} = 2. \tag{4.21}$$

If

$$qu'(2) + 2(1-q)u'(4) < 2 - q,$$

then we may assume that consumer 2 chooses

$$x_{321} = 2 - x_{311}, \tag{4.22}$$

so that supply and demand of capital at the end of period 1 are equated. Note that $u'(2) < 1$ implies the inequality below (4.21) since u' is decreasing.

We conclude that the prices in (4.7)–(4.10) and the quantities in (4.11)–(4.22) constitute an RCE for this example provided that $u'(2) < 1$. Note that, since λ_2 is uncertain at date 1 and consumption of consumer 1 at date 2 is proportional to λ_2 [see Equation (4.12)], consumer 1 faces uncertainty about his future consumption in this RCE. It is easy to show [see Exercise (4.6)] that any Pareto optimal allocation in this economy involves

$$x_{111} = x_{112}(1) = x_{112}(2),$$

that is, full insurance and smoothing of consumption over time for consumer 1. Therefore, the RCE is not Pareto optimal in this environment. The problem is that, since the two consumers are different, there are gains to trade between them that cannot be realized by trading only in consumption goods and capital goods for delivery in the current period. In particular, in period 1 these consumers would like to trade contingent claims for consumption in period 2. The RCE framework allows one to purchase, in period 1, claims for consumption in period 2 only indirectly by purchasing capital goods for delivery at the end of period 1. This provides only for consumption in period 2 that is proportional to λ_2. Thus, the only way to insure fully one's consumption in period 2, trading only the goods available in the RCE framework, is to consume nothing in period 2. This, however, will not generally be either Pareto optimal or equilibrium behavior. Note that the valuation equilibrium framework described in Chapter 3 provides for a complete set of contingent claims, so that any valuation equilibrium for this example would be Pareto optimal.

Because of the suboptimality of the RCE in models with heterogeneous consumers, the RCE appears to be a tool useful for models involving a representative consumer or in which one can exogeneously rule out contingent claims other than those provided by the capital goods in the RCE framework. In such cases, however, the RCE is generally easier to analyze and delivers potentially estimable policy functions and prices more closely related to those we observe than the valuation equilibrium.

EXERCISES

4.1. Check that all the conditions required for a unique, continuous, bounded solution w^* of (4.2) and optimal policy $\delta^*(k,\lambda)$ to exist are satisfied. [See Chapter 2. Also note that since u is continuous, $M(S)$ can be assumed to contain only bounded continuous functions. This set of functions is complete under the norm used in Chapter 2.]

4.2. Use Assumption 4.6 to show that w^* is concave and strictly increasing in k.

4.3. Show that Assumptions 4.1–4.6 hold for Lucas' (1978) model.

4.4. Show that, if the Pareto optimal production vector y^* solves the consumer's problem and the profit maximization problem of firm j in the Lucas (1978) model, then prices must be such that $p_1^* > 0$ and $p_{2j}^* = p_{3j}^* + \lambda_j$.

4.5. Show that the operator T_j defined by the right-hand side of (4.6) maps the set of bounded, continuous functions $f : \mathbf{R}_+^n \to \mathbf{R}_+$ into itself. Also show that T_j is a contraction (this is a good review of Chapter 2).

4.6. For the heterogeneous-consumer example of Section 4.2, show that, for any Pareto optimal allocation, consumer 1's consumption in periods 1 and 2 will be the same, regardless of the realization of λ_2.

NOTES

1. Even if a firm could store capital goods across periods, its profit maximization problem would still be static since the firm faces no budget constraint, and the opportunity cost of using the capital for production would be the same as that of purchasing it at the beginning of the period. Thus a firm is not constrained by how much capital it saves, nor is its profit function affected. For a consumer, however, because of the budget constraint, the amount of capital stored affects consumption possibilities in all future periods.
2. The definition of an RCE is extended in the obvious way to this economy.

REFERENCES

Bewley, T., "The Martingale Property of Asset Prices," CMSEMS discussion paper #431, Northwestern University, June 1980.

Lucas, R. E., Jr., "Asset Prices in an Exchange Economy," *Econometrica,* **46** (1978), pp. 1426–1446.

Prescott, E. C. and R. Mehra, "Recursive Competitive Equilibrium: The Case of Homogeneous Households," *Econometrica,* **48** (1980), pp. 1365–1379.

CHAPTER 5

Equilibria of
Sequential Games

In this chapter, we discuss some tools for analyzing games involving a sequence of moves (sometimes called games in "extensive form") in which players may have different information. The emphasis is on applying these tools to the problem of characterizing mechanisms (we use the term mechanism to mean any extensive form game) and their allocations for efficiently allocating resources in such asymmetric information environments. We first consider an equilibrium concept for extensive form games called "Sequential Equilibrium" [Kreps and Wilson (1982)]. We then use this concept to establish the "Revelation Principle" and apply it to the characterization of efficient mechanisms.

5.1 SEQUENTIAL EQUILIBRIUM[1]

We introduce the concept of Sequential Equilibrium using the following simple example. There are two firms called "Leader" and "Follower." Each is about to build a new plant that can be one of two sizes—small or large. Leader must choose a plant size first, but he has private information regarding the state of demand. In particular, it is known by both firms that demand can be either "high," with probability p, or "low," with probability $1 - p$, but, in addition, Leader knows the true state of demand before choosing his plant size. The payoffs to each firm as functions of the state of demand and the plant sizes chosen by the two firms are given in Table 5.1 (the first number in each pair is the payoff to Leader, the second is the payoff to Follower).

The structure of the game is depicted in the "tree" diagram of Figure 5.1. In this diagram, the dashed lines connecting two nodes at which Follower moves indicate that he cannot tell which of the two nodes is his

Table 5.1 Payoffs in the "Leader-Follower" Game

High Demand Payoffs			
		Leader	
		Large Plant	Small Plant
Follower { Large Plant		(2,1)	(0,1)
Small Plant		(4,0)	(1,0)

Low Demand Payoffs			
		Leader	
		Large Plant	Small Plant
Follower { Large Plant		(0,−1)	(−1,1)
Small Plant		(1,−1)	(2,2)

true "location" when he moves (each such pair of nodes is called an "information set" for Follower). This reflects the assumption that Follower does not know whether demand will be high or low before he must choose his plant size. Either pair of nodes connected by a dashed line is called an "information set" for Follower. The two "open" nodes represent the two possible initial situations corresponding to the two possible starting moves of "Nature." Next to each is indicted (in braces) the probability that that node is the true state of nature.

The main question to be addressed in this example is how can we predict the outcome of the above game. One answer to this question is as follows.

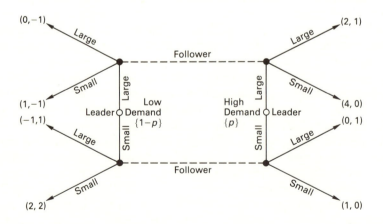

Fig. 5.1 Game tree for the "Leader–Follower" example.

Start with Follower's move, and first suppose that Leader chose a large plant at the previous stage. Clearly, Follower's optimal move in this situation depends on what he believes about the state of demand. This, in turn, depends on his prior beliefs about demand (summarized by p) and *what he can infer from the fact that Leader chose a large plant.* Suppose Follower infers that demand is surely high. Then his best move is clearly to build a large plant (in which case his payoff is 1 as opposed to 0 if he builds a small plant). At this point we have no reason to think that such an inference on the part of Follower is, in any sense, optimal, however, later we will justify this belief. Next suppose that Leader chose a small plant. Further suppose that Follower infers from this move that demand is surely low. Now Follower's optimal choice is to build a small plant. Thus, *given the beliefs, conditioned on Leader's move, previously described,* Follower's optimal move is to build the same size plant as Leader.

Now consider Leader's optimal choice of plant size. Suppose he takes as given the fact that Follower will emulate his decision. Then Leader will optimally choose a large plant if demand is high (his payoff is 2 versus 1 if he chooses small) and a small plant otherwise (his payoff is 2 versus 0 if he chooses small).

Note that we have constructed a consistent set of strategies and beliefs. In particular, Follower's beliefs that demand is surely high (respectively, low) if Leader chooses a large (respectively, small) plant are justified by Leader's strategy. Moreover, Follower's strategy is optimal given his beliefs and Leader's strategy, and Leader's strategy is optimal given his information and Follower's strategy. It is essentially these properties that define a sequential equilibrium (see the formal definition following).

The equilibrium just constructed is not, however, the only possible sequential equilibrium for this game. There is a second equilibrium that illustrates an additional aspect of the sequential equilibrium notion. To construct this equilibrium, let us again consider Follower's move given that Leader has chosen "large." This time, however, let us suppose that Follower infers nothing from Leader's choice, that is, he continues to assign probability p to high demand. Regardless of p, Follower will still find it optimal to choose a large plant in this case. Now suppose Leader has chosen "small," and, again, Follower infers nothing. If $p > 0.5$, then it is optimal for Follower to choose "large" in this case also. Assuming that $p > 0.5$, consider Leader's problem, given that Follower will choose "large" regardless of Leader's choice. Clearly, it is now optimal for Leader to choose "large" regardless of the state of demand. Thus our candidate for a second equilibrium of this game is: Leader always chooses a large plant, Follower infers nothing from Leader's choice (i.e., his posterior beliefs are the same as his priors), and Follower always chooses a large plant.

In order to verify that this is indeed a sequential equilibrium, we need only check that Follower's beliefs following Leader's move are "rational" for *each of Leader's possible moves.* We must verify Follower's beliefs for each of Leader's possible moves, even though in equilibrium we contend that he will always choose "large," because these beliefs determine what Follower *would* do if Leader chose small. Follower's choice in this event is important because it affects Leader's choice. Now, if Leader chooses "large" as expected, then Follower cannot rationally infer anything from this choice since he believes Leader will choose large in either state of demand. If Leader chooses "small," however, we have a problem. Since Follower put no probability on this event *a priori,* he cannot use Bayes' rule to update his beliefs. Normally, we consider beliefs rational if they follow Bayes's rule. In this case, we must create a new definition of rational beliefs. The approach used by Kreps and Wilson is as follows. First perturb Leader's strategy so that it puts positive probability on both "small" and "large" in at least one state of demand. Now, using the *perturbed* strategy, Bayes' rule can be used to calculate posteriors for Follower conditional on either choice by Leader. Next, take the limit of these new posterior beliefs as the magnitude of the perturbation in Leader's strategy approaches zero. The candidate equilibrium beliefs are rational if the posterior beliefs derived from the perturbed strategy converge to the candidate equilibrium beliefs.

To apply this approach, consider the perturbation of Leader's strategy in which he chooses "small" with probability ε and "large" with probability $1 - \varepsilon$, independent of the state of demand. It is easy to see that, given this strategy by Leader, Bayes' rule results in posterior beliefs for Follower that coincide with his prior, regardless of Leader's observed choice of plant size and regardless of ε. Thus, if we take the limit of these posteriors as ε approaches zero (and the perturbed strategy of Leader approaches the candidate equilibrium strategy), we obtain exactly the candidate equilibrium beliefs of Follower. This completes the verification that our candidate equilibrium is, in fact, a sequential equilibrium (see Exercise 5.1).

Note that there are other ways we could have perturbed Leader's strategy in which the resulting posterior would not have converged to the prior. For example, consider the perturbation that Leader chooses "large" for sure if demand is high but chooses "small" with probability ε if demand is low. This might be considered a more "plausible" perturbation. In this case, Bayes' rule results in the posterior belief that demand is high with probability $p/[p + (1 - p)(1 - \varepsilon)]$ if Leader chooses "large" and probability 0 if he chooses "small." As ε approaches zero, the perturbed strategy converges to the candidate equilibrium strategy, but the beliefs converge to the prior if Leader chooses "large" and to low demand for sure if he chooses "small."

With these beliefs for Follower, the given strategies (in which both

Leader and Follower always choose "large") are no longer optimal against each other. In particular, if demand is low and leader were to choose "small," then, given the new beliefs, Follower would believe that demand is low. His optimal response would be "small." Moreover, given that Follower will choose "small," Leader prefers to choose "small" in the low demand state. Thus by changing the off-equilibrium-path beliefs of Follower, we can "destroy" an equilibrium. This suggests that, if beliefs can be further constrained by imposing some additional rationality condition on them, it may be possible to rule out some "undesirable" sequential equilibria.

There are several ways in which off-equilibrium-path beliefs may be constrained. One possible restriction is that the perturbations be such that the candidate equilibrium strategies are optimal against the perturbed strategies (given beliefs derived from those strategies using Bayes' rule). Sequential equilibria with this property are called "perfect" [or sometimes "trembling hand perfect;" see Selten (1975)]. It turns out that adding this restriction doesn't affect things much, as is shown in Theorem 5.4 discussed later.

Another approach to reducing the set of sequential equilibria is to rule out certain off-equilibrium-path beliefs directly. In the preceding example of Figure 5.1, consider again the equilibrium in which Leader always chooses "large," Follower's beliefs always coincide with his prior (even if Leader chooses "small"), and Follower also always chooses "large." If demand were really low, and if Leader could convince Follower of this fact by choosing "small" (or at least persuade him that demand is low with probability at least 0.5), then Leader would be better off than in the proposed equilibrium. In this case, Follower would choose "small," and Leader would receive a payoff of two instead of a payoff of zero. On the other hand, if demand were really high, it would not be to Leader's advantage to convince Follower that demand were low by choosing "small." Therefore, if Leader chooses "small," an event with probability zero given the proposed equilibrium, Follower can reason as follows. If, by choosing, "small," Leader is trying to convince me that demand is high (or that it is high with probability $p > 0.5$), then Leader is irrational, because, even if I believe him, I will choose "large," and he will be worse off, no matter the true state of demand, than if he had stuck with the equilibrium strategy. On the other hand, if he is trying to convince me that demand is low, and I believe him, he will be better off if demand really is low but worse off otherwise. Therefore, it makes sense for me to believe that demand is low after observing Leader's choice of "small," but it does not make sense for me to believe that demand is high (or to stick with my prior). Thus, in a sense, it is not rational for Follower to stick with his prior beliefs if Leader deviates from the equilibrium strategy by choosing "small," even though the prior is the limit of Bayesian beliefs derived from properly perturbed strategies. In this way, the proposed equilibrium, although sequential, can be eliminated. This idea can, of course, be generalized, although we will not pursue the general case here.[2]

In order to define sequential equilibrium formally and state some results concerning it, we will need to introduce some notation and concepts. First, we will define a game among a finite set of players, I, by giving its tree structure: a finite set of "nodes," each labeled by the name of the player who moves at that node, a set of shared probability beliefs about which of the initial nodes was chosen by "nature" (initial probabilities are shown next to the initial node in braces), a set of arrows between the nodes showing to which node the game moves from any given node for each move allowed to the player who moves at the given node, a set of "dashed lines," each connecting two or more nodes, representing the set of nodes among which the player who moves at those nodes cannot distinguish (such a set of nodes is called an "information set" for that player), and a utility payoff to each player at each final node. The initial probability beliefs are denoted by $\rho(w)$, where w denotes an initial node, and the utility payoff of player i by $u^i(z)$, where z denotes a terminal node. In terms of the example of Figure 5.1, $\rho(\text{high demand}) = p$, $\rho(\text{low demand}) = 1 - p$, and the u^i are given in Table 5.1 (e.g., if z is the terminal node corresponding to high demand and both players choosing small plants, then $u^L(z) = 2$ and $u^F(z) = 1$, where L and F stand for Leader and Follower, respectively).

A *strategy* for a player i is simply a random choice of a feasible action (arrow) at each information set at which he must move. (We think of a player as moving at an information set instead of at a node, since he cannot tell apart the various nodes in an information set, and, therefore, his strategy cannot be different for different nodes within an information set.) Such a strategy is denoted by $\pi^i(h)$, where h is an information set, that is, for each h at which i moves, $\pi^i(h)$ assigns a probability to each action that can be chosen at that information set. Naturally, these probabilities must be nonnegative and sum to one at each information set. A *strategy vector*, π, is a vector whose components are the π^i, $i \in I$. The set of all feasible strategy vectors is denoted by Π.

A *proper subform* of a game tree is a node together with that part of the tree which emanates from that node. If, for each node in the subform, all the other nodes that are in the information set of that node are also in the subform, then the subform is called a *proper subgame* (the initial beliefs assign probability one to the single initial node). Note that if, for some node in a subform, there are nodes in the information set of that node that are not in the subform, then it doesn't make sense to call the subform a subgame of the original game.

The starting point for defining sequential equilibrium is the familiar concept of Nash equilibrium, that is, a strategy vector $\pi \in \Pi$ is a Nash

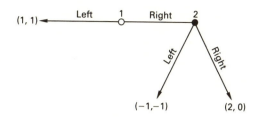

Fig. 5.2 Example for subgame perfection.

equilibrium if, for each player $i \in I$,

$$E^{\pi}[u^i(z)] \geqslant E^{\pi'}[u^i(z)] \quad \text{for all } \pi' \in \Pi \text{ such that } \pi'^j = \pi^j \text{ for } j \neq i.$$

In this expression, E^{π} denotes the expectation with respect to the distribution induced on final nodes, z, by the prior ρ and the strategy vector π. One problem with this concept, however, is that, in many cases it allows "too many" equilibria. Moreover, many of these equilibria may be nonsensical as the example in Figure 5.2 [taken from Kreps and Wilson (1982, Figure 2, p. 869)] illustrates.

One Nash equilibrium of this game is for player 1 to choose Left and for player 2, if he gets a chance to move, to choose Left as well. Given that player 1 will choose Left for sure, player 2's choice of Left is optimal. If player 1 were to choose Right, however, it would make no sense for player 2 to choose Left (unless he can somehow "precommit" himself). If player 1 realizes this he "should choose" Right, that is, player 2's "threat" to choose Left is not credible. To rule out such Nash equilibria, Selten (1965) has proposed the following refinement of Nash equilibrium.

Definition 5.1 Strategy vector π is *subgame perfect* if, for every proper subgame, the strategy π restricted to the subgame constitutes a Nash equilibrium for the subgame.

If we believe that Nash equilibrium is a good description of the way people behave in game situations, then surely they should continue to behave in that way in any subgame (unless they can commit themselves, before reaching the subgame, to some other behavior). It is clear that the refinement of subgame perfection rules out the "nonsensical" Nash equilibrium in the example of Figure 5.2. The only subgame perfect strategy vector has both players choosing Right.

Although the concept of subgame perfection can be applied only to proper subgames, the idea of consistency embodied in subgame perfection can be applied more broadly, as the example of Fig. 5.3 shows [the example is taken from Kreps and Wilson (1982, Figure 4, p. 871)]. One Nash equilibrium of this game is for player 1 to choose Across and player 2

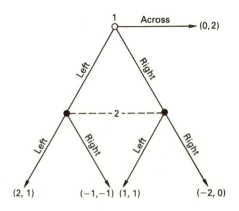

Fig. 5.3 Example for sequential rationality.

to choose Right. Since the only proper subgame of this game is the game itself (because the entire information set of player 2 is not included in any proper subform), this equilibrium is also subgame perfect. The problem with this equilibrium is, as in the previous example, that player 2's strategy makes sense, given the strategy of player 1, only because player 2 is sure that he will not get the opportunity to move. Subgame perfection cannot be applied to rule out this equilibrium because there is no probability assessment for the two nodes in player 2's information set which can be derived from the original game. Thus, there is no way to calculate player 2's expected utility for each of his moves. Nevertheless, it is clear that, no matter what probabilities one assigns to the two nodes in player 2's information set, player 2 prefers Left if he gets a chance to move. This suggests that we could apply the basic idea embodied in subgame perfection to a wider set of situations if we had some natural way of assigning probability beliefs to nodes in information sets. In that case, we could rule out strategies that were not "sequentially rational," that is, those not optimal for the "subgame" defined using those beliefs and given the strategies of the other players.

   To define the beliefs of players regarding nodes in their information sets in a natural way, we incorporate these beliefs in the definition of equilibrium. A *system of beliefs,* is defined as a mapping μ that assigns a probability to each node in each information set. These probabilities are interpreted as the probabilities assigned to the nodes in the information set by the player whose information set it is, if that information set is reached. An *assessment* is defined as a pair (μ, π) consisting of a system of beliefs and a strategy vector. Given such an assessment, conditional probabilities of the final nodes, given that a particular information set has been reached, are defined in the obvious way. With these beliefs, optimal strategies are simply strategies that maximize conditional expected utility for the final nodes, given that a particular information set has been reached. More formally, an assessment (μ, π) is *sequentially rational* if for any information set h and any strategy vector π' such that $\pi^j = \pi'^j$ for $j \neq i$,

$$E^{\mu, \pi}[u^i(z) \mid h] \geq E^{\mu, \pi'}[u^i(z) \mid h],$$

where i is the player who moves at information set h and $E^{\mu, \pi}$ is the expectation over final nodes, z, using the probability distribution induced by the assessment (μ, π). Sequential equilibrium will be defined in terms of assessments, not just in terms of strategies.

The basic idea of sequential equilibrium is that a system of beliefs about where one is in the game tree, together with a strategy for each player, jointly constitute an equilibrium if the strategies are optimal given the beliefs and the strategies of other players, and the beliefs satisfy Bayes' rule (when applicable). In order to define the concept formally, we must introduce some additional notation. Let Π_0 be the set of all strictly positive strategy vectors, that is, those strategy vectors that put positive probability on each possible action at each node. Such strategy vectors are important because, if such a strategy vector is being followed, then, no matter at what information set a player finds himself, that set has positive probability of being reached given the strategy vector. Consequently, the player can update his beliefs about his current location in the game tree by using Bayes' rule to compute the conditional probability of any node in the current information set given the fact that that information set has been reached. Thus, for strictly positive strategy vectors, the only sensible way to define a system of beliefs is

$$\mu(x) = P^\pi(x)/P^\pi(H(x)), \tag{5.1}$$

where $P^\pi(x)$ is the probability of reaching node x given the strategy vector π, and $H(x)$ is the information set containing x. Note that μ "correctly" (in the sense of Bayes' rule) extracts the information that can be inferred from knowing what strategy one's opponents are following and observing their actual choices.

While this procedure for constructing systems of beliefs works well for strictly positive strategy vectors, problems may arise when the strategy vector is not positive. In particular, how does one sensibly define beliefs at an information set that has zero probability of being reached given the strategy vector?[3] The resolution of this problem embodied in the definition of sequential equilibrium is to call beliefs rational in such a situation if they are "close to" Bayesian beliefs defined relative to a strategy vector that is "close to" the given vector. More formally, we say that an assessment (μ, π) is *consistent* if

$$(\mu, \pi) = \lim_{n \to \infty} (\mu_n, \pi_n),$$

where, for each n, $\pi_n \in \Pi_0$ and μ_n is calculated from π_n (and ρ) using Bayes' rule, that is, μ_n and π_n satisfy (5.1). The sequence $\{(\mu_n, \pi_n)\}$ is said to *justify* the assessment (μ, π). We may now define sequential equilibrium:

Definition 5.2 A *sequential equilibrium* is an assessment (μ, π) that is both consistent and sequentially rational.

Four general results of interest to us can be proved for sequential equilibrium (see Kreps and Wilson (1982) for proof).

Theorem 5.1 For every extensive form game, there exists at least one sequential equilibrium.

Theorem 5.2 If (μ, π) is a sequential equilibrium, then π is a subgame perfect Nash equilibrium.

The third result concerns the relationship between sequential equilibrium and Selten's (1975) concept of "perfect equilibrium" (sometimes called "trembling hand perfection" and not to be confused with "subgame perfection" described above). In order to state this result, we must first define "perfect equilibrium." The basic idea is to require that, in order to be a perfect equilibrium strategy vector, the strategy of each player must continue to be optimal even when the other players' strategies are perturbed for at least some set of perturbations which puts positive probability on all actions. This eliminates equilibria involving "idle threats" (i.e., one which a player would not want to carry out if he actually reached the node at which he had the chance to carry it out, but which is optimal only because the node will never be reached). Such threats would not remain optimal in the face of any perturbation which resulted in strictly positive strategies. Formally, we have

Definition 5.3 An assessment (μ, π) is a *perfect equilibrium* if it is justified by a sequence $\{(\mu_n, \pi_n)\}$ for which, for each player i and each index n, π^i is an optimal response for player i, given beliefs μ_n, to the other players' strategies π_n^j for $j \neq i$.

Note that if π^i is a best response to π_n for each n, then π^i is a best response to π. This makes apparent the third general result.

Theorem 5.3 Every perfect equilibrium is a sequential equilibrium.

The converse of Theorem 5.3 is false as is shown by the game depicted in Figure 5.4 [this example is taken from Kreps and Wilson (1982, Figure 13, p. 883)]. In this game, one sequential equilibrium involves player 1 choosing Left for sure and player 2 choosing Right for sure (beliefs at player 2's information set are that the game is at node x with probability

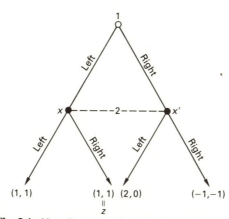

Fig. 5.4 Not all sequential equilibria are perfect.

one). This is not perfect because if player 2 believes player 1 puts any probability, no matter how small, on Right, then player 2 will prefer to choose Left. Note that the example depends on the fact, that, given that player 1 chooses Left, player 2 is indifferent between Left and Right. It turns out that if we consider only equilibria that are "strict" (see the precise definition which follows), and if we allow substitution of approximately equal payoffs for the actual payoffs, we can assume perfection.

More formally, a sequential equilibrium (μ,π) is *strict* if for any two actions between which some player i is indifferent, π^i puts strictly positive probability on both actions. The following result is shown in Kreps and Wilson (1982, Theorem 3 and following discussion).

Theorem 5.4 Consider any fixed extensive form game with payoffs u, and sequential equilibrium (μ,π). Then for any neighborhood of u (no matter how small), there is a payoff vector u' in that neighborhood such that (μ,π) is a strict sequential equilibrium of the new game formed by replacing u with u' in the original game, and (μ,π) is perfect.

Theorem 5.4 can be applied to the example of Figure 5.4: if we change the payoff vector at the terminal node following the moves Left then Right from $(1,1)$ to $(1,1+\varepsilon)$ for any $\varepsilon > 0$, then the sequential equilibrium previously described is perfect. To see this, note that if player 1 were to choose Right with probability $1/n$, $n > 0$, player 2's beliefs would be that he is at node x with probability $(1 - 1/n)$ and at node x' with probability $1/n$. Thus, given this perturbed strategy of player 1, player 2's expected utility if he chooses Right exceeds that if he chooses Left for all $n > (1 + \varepsilon)/\varepsilon$. Consequently, the sequence of assessments given by

$$\pi_n^1(\text{Right}) = 1/n, \quad \pi_n^1(\text{Left}) = 1 - 1/n, \quad \pi_n^2(\text{Right}) = 1, \quad \pi_n^2(\text{Left}) = 0,$$
$$\mu_n^2(x) = 1 - 1/n, \quad \mu_n^2(x') = 1/n \quad \text{for} \quad n > (1 + \varepsilon)/\varepsilon,$$

justifies the sequential equilibrium assessment and is such that Right with probability one is optimal for player 2 against π_n given μ_n.

This concludes our discussion of sequential equilibium. In the next section, we show how this concept can be used to derive the "revelation principle."

5.2 EFFICIENT MECHANISMS AND THE "REVELATION PRINCIPLE"[4]

Our main purpose in this section is to develop a tool that can be used to characterize efficient mechanisms and efficient allocations in asymmetric information environments. This tool, which has been called the "Revelation Principle," states that, in searching for an efficient mechanism, one may restrict attention to a class of particularly simple mechanisms called "revelation games." In a revelation game, each agent is asked to reveal whatever relevant information is in his possession. These revelations (which need not be truthful) then determine an allocation of resources (or a set of payoffs to the agents). We begin with a simple example [taken from Harris and Townsend (1981, Section 2)].

Consider an environment consisting of two agents, an employer (denoted by the subscript e) and a worker (denoted by the subscript w). The worker may supply any amount of effort $z \geqslant 0$ to a production process. The output of this process is

$$y = \theta z, \tag{5.2}$$

where θ is a productivity parameter. The employer may not supply effort. The worker's preferences over consumption c and effort z are defined by the utility function

$$u_w(c,z) = c - z^2. \tag{5.3}$$

The employer's preferences over consumption are defined by the utility function

$$u_e(c) = c. \tag{5.4}$$

The worker is assumed to have observed the value of the productivity parameter θ before any trade takes place between him and the employer. This information is private, that is, the employer cannot observe θ. He believes that θ is drawn from the following distribution: $\theta = a$ with probability p and $\theta = b$ with probability $1 - p$, where $0 < a < b$. In addition, the employer is assumed to be unable to observe the worker's input, z. Otherwise, since output, y, will be observable, the employer could infer θ. All information, other than the value of θ and w's choice of z, is common knowledge, including preferences and the fact that the worker knows the value of θ.

An allocation in this environment can be interpreted as a reward, r, and an output quota, y, for the worker. Thus, given a value θ of the productivity parameter, preferences over allocations induced by the technology in (5.2) and the preferences in (5.3) and (5.4) are given by the utility functions

$$U_w(y,r,\theta) = r - [y/\theta]^2 \qquad (5.5)$$

and

$$U_e(y,r,\theta) = y - r. \qquad (5.6)$$

Indifference curves of the utility functions in (5.5) and (5.6) are depicted in Figure 5.5. Notice that the worker's utility function depends directly on the parameter θ. The indifference curve of the worker corresponding to the higher value of θ, $\theta = b$, is flatter at any point than the curve corresponding to $\theta = a$ at that point. Indifference curves of the employer are simply 45-degree lines. Utility of the worker increases with r and decreases with y, while utility of the employer decreases with r and increases with y. The set of feasible (y,r) pairs is the area under the 45-degree line through the origin, where $0 \leqslant r \leqslant y$. The actual allocation achieved in this environment could be contingent on the value of θ, that is, r and y may be functions of θ. Such allocations are called "parameter-contingent" or simply "contingent" allocations. Since θ can take on only two values in this example,

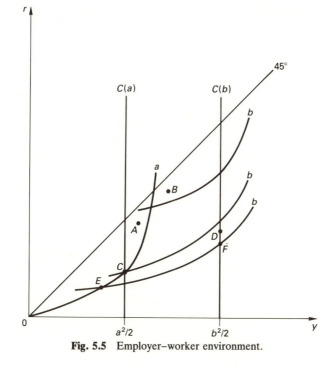

Fig. 5.5   Employer–worker environment.

contingent allocations can be represented graphically in Figure 5.5 by *pairs* of points, for example, (A,B).

A number of general points can be made with this simple example. The first is that contingent allocations that do not satisfy a certain "incentive-compatibility" property cannot be achieved. This property is that the worker must prefer the allocation $[y(a),r(a)]$ to $[y(b),r(b)]$ when, in fact, $\theta = a$, and vice versa when $\theta = b$. Mathematically, incentive-compatibility or "IC" for this example is defined by

$$r(a) - [y(a)/a]^2 \geqslant r(b) - [y(b)/a]^2, \tag{5.7}$$
$$r(b) - [y(b)/b]^2 \geqslant r(a) - [y(a)/b]^2. \tag{5.8}$$

A contingent allocation that satisfies IC is shown in Figure 5.5 as the pair of points (A,B), where $A = [y(a),r(a)]$ and $B = [y(b),r(b)]$. The reason that a contingent allocation that does not satisfy IC cannot be achieved is simple. The only way that an allocation can actually depend on the true value of θ is if, somehow, either directly or indirectly, the worker reveals this value during the allocation process (remember, only he observes θ). Knowing this, the worker will reveal θ if and only if he prefers the outcome associated with its true value to the one associated with its other possible value. Thus, either the contingent allocation actually achieved by the allocation process does not depend on θ, in which case it satisfies IC trivially, or the worker prefers the outcome associated with the true value of θ to the one associated with the other value, in which case the contingent allocation also satisfies IC.

Note that this is an "if and only if" argument. Thus we see that, not only are "non-IC" allocations impossible to achieve, IC allocations can be achieved. In fact, IC allocations can be achieved simply by asking the worker to reveal the true value of θ with the understanding that the given contingent allocation will be effected as a function of the worker's reported value of θ. In such a mechanism, since the allocation satisfies IC, the worker has no incentive to lie. We have sketched a "proof" of the Revelation Principle for this example: any achievable allocation in this environment is the allocation corresponding to a truthful equilibrium of a revelation game.

Next, consider the notion of what is an optimal allocation in this example. If the value of θ were public information, then, for each realization of θ, an optimal allocation would equate the marginal product of labor, θ, with the worker's marginal disutility of labor $2z$. That is, if θ were known to be, say, a, an efficient allocation would have $z = a/2$ or $y = a^2/2$. Similarly, if $\theta = b$, an efficient allocation would have $y = b^2/2$. The worker's reward r does not enter in this case: it is simply the means by which the optimal output is distributed. The set of "full-information" efficient allocations in this case is simply a vertical line at $y = \theta^2/2$. These two "full-information contract curves" are shown in Figure 5.5 as $C(a)$ and $C(b)$ for $\theta = a$ and $\theta = b$, respectively. One might conjecture that any contingent allocation in which $y(\theta) = \theta^2/2$, for each value of θ would be an optimal contingent allocation in this environment. In fact, however, this is not the case. The reason is that some full-information- (or FI-) optimal contingent allocations are not achievable because they do not satisfy IC.[5] An example is given in Figure 5.5 by the pair of points (C,D).

A related point that can be made with the example just discussed is that there are contingent allocations that are optimal in an "ex ante" sense, but that are not FI-optimal. First, we define a feasible contingent allocation to be *ex ante optimal* for this example if (i) it satisfies IC, (ii) no other feasible contingent allocation that satisfies IC can make the employer better off in the sense of expected utility taking expectations over θ using his prior beliefs without making the worker worse off for at least one value of θ, and (iii) no other feasible contingent allocation that satisfies IC can make the worker better off for some value of θ without either making him worse off for the other value of θ or making the employer worse off (in the ex ante expected utility sense) or both.

Given this definition, we can find the ex ante optimal contingent allocation that maximizes the employer's ex ante expected utility, given that the worker is not required to work, that is, the worker's utility for each value of θ must satisfy an "individual rationality" (or IR) constraint which guarantees that he will be no worse off than if he does not work (in which case $y = r = 0$) by solving the following program:

$$\max_{[y(\theta),r(\theta)],\ \theta=a,b} p[y(a) - r(a)] + (1 - p)[y(b) - r(b)]$$

subject to (5.7) and (5.8),

$$\text{IR:} \qquad r(\theta) - [y(\theta)/\theta]^2 \geq 0 \quad \text{for } \theta = a,b \quad \text{and}$$

$$\text{Feasibility:} \quad 0 \leq r(\theta) \leq y(\theta) \qquad \text{for } \theta = a,b.$$

Note that, since any solution must satisfy IC, it can be achieved by a revelation game as outlined above.

A typical solution (for a particular value of p) is shown in Figure 5.5 as points (E,F). It can be shown that any solution will have $[y(b),r(b)]$ on $C(b)$ and $[y(a),r(a)]$ such that the worker is indifferent between $[y(a),r(a)]$ and $(0,0)$ when $\theta = a$. Since E is not on $C(a)$, this solution is not *FI*-optimal. Since the true value of θ is revealed by any allocation process that achieves the allocation (E,F), if $\theta = a$, there will be gains to trade ex post. The contingent allocation (E,F) is ex ante optimal in the sense that the two players have an incentive to agree ex ante not to exploit any ex post gains to trade. If such commitments cannot be enforced, then (E,F) is not a feasible outcome. It is assumed throughout this section that this kind of commitment is possible.[6]

Finally, note that the solution depends on the employer's prior beliefs about θ, that is, on p, the probability that $\theta = a$. As this probability increases, the employer's expected utility can be improved by giving him more consumption in the state $\theta = a$. This is accomplished, without decreasing the worker's utility in that state, by moving E along the worker's indifference curve through E corresponding to $\theta = a$ toward the point C. In order to satisfy IC, F must move up along $C(b)$, that is, the employer must give up utility in the event that $\theta = a$. His expected utility still increases because the probability of this event has decreased (p has increased). Note that the worker's utility in the event $\theta = b$ increases as F moves up along $C(b)$.

This concludes our discussion of the employer–worker example. We now consider general economic models that satisfy the following assumptions. There is a finite set T of agents denoted by the subscript t. Each has the same consumption possibility set C, which is a subset of $\mathbf{R}_+^\ell$, where ℓ is the (finite) number of commodities. Preferences of each agent t are defined by a utility function, $U_t : C \times \Theta \to \mathbf{R}$, where

$$\Theta = \prod_{k \in N} \Theta_k$$

is the set of possible values of a parameter vector $\theta = (\theta_1, \ldots, \theta_n)$, $\theta_k \in \Theta_k$, Θ_k finite, $N = \{1, \ldots, n\}$. We assume that more consumption is preferred to less, that is, that U_t is increasing in c.

The production technology is modeled by assuming that associated with each coalition of agents $A \subset T$, there is a production possibility set $\lambda(A) \subset C^A$. The set $\lambda(A)$ specifies the set of feasible allocations to agents in A using only the resources available to A, that is, the set of vectors of consumption bundles $c^A = (c_a)$ for $a \in A$ that the coalition A can achieve on its own. We refer to the mapping λ as the "technology" of the economy and assume that the allocation that assigns zero to all agents is feasible for any coalition, that is, $0^A \in \lambda(A)$ for every coalition A. A *parameter–contingent* (contingent) allocation is a possibly random allocation which depends on the value of θ, that is, a mapping Q from Θ into the set of distributions on $\lambda(T)$. Thus $Q(c^T \mid \theta)$ is interpreted as the probability that the allocation is $\leq c^T \in \lambda(T)$, given θ.

Finally, the economy must include a specification of the information structure. It is assumed that the utility functions U_t, $t \in T$, the parameter space Θ, and the technology λ are all common knowledge. Each agent t is assumed to observe a subvector $\theta^t = (\theta_k)$, $k \in N^t$, of the parameter vector θ, where $N^t \subset N$. Note that if two agents s and t observe the same parameter, then $N^t \cap N^s$ is nonempty. We assume that each parameter is observed by at least one agent, that is,

$$\bigcup_{t \in T} N^t = N.$$

Agent t's beliefs about the value of the full parameter vector θ are given by a distribution $\rho_t: \Theta \times \Theta^t \to [0,1]$, where $\rho_t(\theta \mid \theta^t)$ is interpreted as the probability that the parameter vector has the value θ, given that t has observed θ^t. The sets N^t and the distribution functions ρ_t for $t \in T$ are also common knowledge. Thus each agent knows which parameters are observed by each other agent. Expectations with respect to the distribution ρ_t are denoted $E_t(\cdot \mid \theta^t)$.

In the employer–worker example, the set of agents $T = \{e, w\}$, the consumption possibility set is $C = \mathbf{R}_+^2$, the technology is $\lambda(\{e\}) = \lambda(\{w\}) = \{(0,0)\}$ and $\lambda(T) = \{(y,r) \in C \mid r \leq y\}$, and the utility functions are given by

$$U_e(y,r,\theta) = y - r,$$
$$U_w(y,r,\theta) = r - (y/\theta)^2.$$

Also $N = \{1\}$, $\Theta = \{a,b\}$ and the information structure is $N^e = \varnothing$ and $N^w = \{1\}$, $\rho_e(a) = p$, $\rho_e(b) = 1 - p$, and $\rho_w(\theta \mid \theta^w) = 1$ if $\theta^w = \theta$ and 0 otherwise for $\theta = a, b$.

The class of models to which the analysis applies are those that can be formalized using the above framework. Although this includes a very broad range of economic environments, there are some important restrictions embodied in the framework. First, notice that the technology λ cannot depend on the parameter vector θ. To see the importance of this assumption, suppose that some allocation procedure specifies that, given the behavior of the agents, a particular allocation c should be effected. If λ is allowed to depend on θ, it may be the case that, given the true values of the parameters, c is not feasible. In this case, the allocation procedure is not well defined. Thus, if the technology is allowed to depend on θ, one must restrict allocation mechanisms to specify only allocations which are feasible for all values of θ.[7] For example, in the employer–worker environment, suppose we add the restriction that effort $z \leq 1$. Thus $\lambda(T)$ becomes $\lambda(T,\theta) = \{(r,y) \in C \mid r \leq y \leq \theta\}$. In order to be sure that an allocation procedure is well defined, one would have to specify that all allocations satisfy $y \leq a$. This would rule out many allocation procedures and allocations that one might reasonably expect to observe in this environment.

The second important restriction embodied in this framework is that no new private information be acquired over time. That is, it is assumed that all private information is specified by the values of any privately observed components of the parameter vector θ. These observations are made before any trade takes place. If additional private information is observed during the evolution of an allocation process, then at earlier stages in the process, agents would be concerned with the extent to which the information revealed by their current behavior also reveals information about their future private observations. This problem has been considered by Townsend (1982).

In what follows, we use the term "mechanism" for an economic environment specified as above to mean any extensive form game (see Section 5.1) for the agents in T. Payoffs in the mechanism are, however, specified as allocations rather than utility payoffs. Thus any mechanism M together with a strategy vector π for the mechanism induces a contingent allocation we denote by $M(\pi)$, that is, $M(\pi)(c^T \mid \theta)$ is the probability that the mechanism will end with an allocation $\leqslant c^T \in \lambda(T)$, given that agents are using the strategy vector π and the true parameter values are those given by θ. An "equilibrium" of a mechanism is a sequential equilibrium (again, see Section 5.1).[8] A revelation game R is simply a game in which each agent t declares a value for the parameter subvector he observes, that is, reports an element of Θ^t. These declarations are made simultaneously after which a prespecified, possibly random allocation is effected. The allocation, say F, maps the vector of declared parameter values, $\theta^T \in \Theta^T$, into a distribution on $\lambda(T)$, where

$$\Theta^T = \prod_{t \in T} \Theta^t.$$

A revelation game is fully characterized by its allocation rule, F.

The results fall into two categories, incentive-compatibility theorems and welfare propositions. We consider first the incentive-compatibility theorems. These state that (i) any contingent allocation induced by any equilibrium strategy vector for any mechanism must satisfy certain incentive-compatibility constraints (see the preceding employer–worker example for an illustration), and (ii) conversely, any contingent allocation that satisfies the incentive-compatibility conditions can be achieved as the truthful equilibrium of a revelation game.

To state these theorems formally, we need some additional notation. For any parameter vector θ and any agent t, let $p_t(\theta^t)$ be the subvector of θ consisting of those parameters that only t observes, that is, his "private" parameters. Let $h_t(\theta)$ be the remaining components of θ, so that $\theta = (p_t(\theta^t), h_t(\theta))$. If Q is a contingent allocation, then for any parameter vector $\delta \in \Theta$, any agent t, and any value of t's observed parameters θ^t, let

$$W_t(Q, \theta^t, \delta^t) = E_t\{E_Q[U_t(c, \theta) \mid (p_t(\delta^t), h_t(\theta))] \mid \theta^t\},$$

where the inner expectation is taken with respect to the distribution defined by Q. Thus W_t is t's expected utility for the contingent allocation Q if the values of t's privately observed parameters used to evaluate Q were changed to those given by δ while all other parameters were kept at their true values. Let V_t denote t's expected utility for Q given that Q is evaluated at the true value of θ, that is,

$$V_t(Q, \theta^t) = W_t(Q, \theta^t, \theta^t).$$

A contingent allocation Q is said to satisfy *incentive-compatibility* (IC) if

$$V_t(Q, \theta^t) \geq W_t(Q, \theta^t, \delta^t) \quad \text{for all } \theta^t, \delta^t \in \Theta^t \text{ and } t \in T. \tag{5.9}$$

Condition (5.9) states that t prefers the contingent allocation that results from evaluating Q at the true value of the parameter vector to that which results from evaluating Q at a parameter vector in which those components observed privately by t have been altered. Finally, if R is a revelation game, let π^τ be the strategy vector that puts probability one on the true value of one's observed parameter vector, that is,

$$\pi_t^\tau(\theta^t)(\delta^t) = 1 \quad \text{if and only if } \theta^t = \delta^t \quad \text{for all } t.$$

We may now state the first result just described.

Theorem 5.5 [Harris–Townsend (1981, p. 46)]. Let M be any mechanism and let π^* be any equilibrium strategy vector for M. Then the contingent allocation $M(\pi^*)$ satisfies IC.

Proof Suppose $M(\pi^*)$ does not satisfy IC. Then for some agent s and for some γ^s and $\delta^s \in \Theta^s$,

$$V_s[M(\pi^*), \gamma^s] < W_s[M(\pi^*), \gamma^s, \delta^s]. \tag{5.10}$$

Consider the strategy vector π that agrees with π^* for agents other than s, but for agent s, π specifies that when $\theta^s = \gamma^s$, agent s should choose the same actions as he would have done using π^* when his private parameters $p_s(\theta^s) = p_s(\delta^s)$, and otherwise he should continue to play π^*. That is,

$$\pi_t(\theta^t) = \pi_t^*(\theta^t) \quad \text{if } t \neq s \text{ or if } t = s \text{ and } \theta^s \neq \gamma^s,$$

$$\pi_s(\gamma^s) = \pi_s^*[p_s(\delta^s), q_s(\gamma^s)],$$

where $q_s(\theta^s)$ is the subvector of θ^s consisting of those components at least one another agent observes.

Let

$$\Theta^{-s} = \prod_{k \notin N^s} \Theta_k,$$

$$\Gamma = \{(\theta^{-s}, \gamma^s) \mid \theta^{-s} \in \Theta^{-s}\},$$

$$\pi_{-s} = (\pi_t), \quad t \neq s.$$

Now, for any $\gamma \in \Gamma$,

$$M(\pi)(\cdot \mid \gamma) = M(\pi^*)[\cdot \mid p_s(\delta^s), h_s(\gamma)].$$

Therefore,

$$V_s[M(\pi), \gamma^s] = W_s[M(\pi^*), \gamma^s, \delta^s].$$

Consequently, by (5.10),

$$V_s[M(\pi^*), \gamma^s] < V_s[M(\pi), \gamma^s].$$

Moreover, for $\theta \notin \Gamma$,

$$V_s[M(\pi^*), \theta^s] = V_s[M(\pi), \theta^s],$$

since in this case $\pi = \pi^*$. This implies, however, that π_s^* is not an optimal strategy for s against π_{-s}^*, that is, that π^* is not an equilibrium strategy vector for M, which contradicts the hypotheses of the Theorem.   Q.E.D.

The intuition for this result is simple. Suppose the true realization of the parameter vector is γ. If agent s prefers the equilibrium outcome of M corresponding to a realization of the parameters in which his privately observed parameters took on the value $p_s(\delta^s)$, while all other parameters continued to have the values given by γ, to the equilibrium outcome corresponding to the true value γ, he can have this outcome simply by playing his equilibrium strategy as if the true realization were $(p_s(\delta^s), h_s(\gamma))$ instead of γ. In this case the actual equilibrium outcome would not be $M(\pi^*)(\cdot \mid \gamma)$ as assumed.

The second result described above is given in

Theorem 5.6 [Harris–Townsend (1981, p. 47)].   Let Q be any contingent allocation that satisfies IC. Then there exists a revelation game R in which π^τ is an equilibrium, and $Q = R(\pi^\tau)$. Moreover, if all parameters are privately observed, then R can be taken to be the revelation game whose allocation rule is Q.

Proof   Since we seek an allocation rule such that π^τ is an equilibrium strategy vector, we are mainly concerned with the allocation given that all agents' reported parameter values agree on components that are observed by more than one of them. In particular, the allocation rule must agree with Q given such a report. Consequently define $K \subset \Theta^T$ to be the set of reports that agree on commonly observed parameters, that is,

$$K = \{\theta^T \in \Theta^T \mid \quad \text{for all } t, s \in T, \ \theta_k^t = \theta_k^s \quad \text{for all } k \in N^t \cap N^s\}.$$

Also, for each $\theta^T \in K$ and $k \in N$, let $\kappa_k(\theta^T) = \theta_k^t$ for any agent t who observes parameters k, that is, for any t such that $k \in N^t$. Let $\kappa(\theta^T) = (\kappa_k(\theta^T))$, $k \in N$.

Define R to be the revelation game whose allocation rule is

$$F(\cdot \mid \theta^T) = \begin{cases} Q(\cdot \mid \kappa(\theta^T)) & \text{if } \theta^T \in K \\ Z(\cdot) & \text{otherwise,} \end{cases}$$

where $Z(\cdot)$ puts probability one on the zero allocation in $\lambda(T)$. Note that, for any $\theta \in \Theta$, $\pi^\tau(\theta) \in K$ and $\kappa[\pi^\tau(\theta)] = \theta$. Therefore, for any θ, $Q(\cdot \mid \theta) = F(\cdot \mid \pi^\tau(\theta))$. We show first that π^τ is an equilibrium strategy vector for R. Consider an arbitrary agent t, and let π_t be a feasible strategy for t. Suppose, for some parameter vector θ, $\pi_t(\theta^t)$ puts positive probability on a report for t's nonprivate parameters which differs from θ. Let $\pi = (\pi_t, \pi_{-t}^\tau)$. Then $R(\pi)$ puts positive probability on Z. Since Z is the worst possible outcome for t, he can improve his expected utility by modifying π_t to put probability one on the true value of the nonprivate parameter vector while continuing to put the same marginal probability distribution on his private parameter vector. Therefore, we need consider only responses to π^τ that put probability one on the true value of the nonprivate parameter vector. Suppose π_t is such a strategy. Then any realization of $\pi = (\pi_t, \pi_{-t}^\tau)$ is an element of K. Therefore, for any θ^t,

$$V_t[R(\pi), \theta^t] = E_{\pi_t}\{W_t[Q, \theta^t, \delta^t]\},$$
$$\leqslant V_t(Q, \theta^t) \quad \text{since } Q \text{ satisfies IC},$$
$$= V_t[R(\pi^\tau), \theta^t] \quad \text{since } Q(\cdot \mid \theta) = F(\cdot \mid \pi^\tau(\theta)),$$

where the expectation in the first equality is taken over δ^t using the distribution given by $\pi_t(\theta^t)$. This proves that π^τ is an equilibrium of R. Since, as noted above, $Q(\cdot \mid \theta) = F(\cdot \mid \pi^\tau(\theta))$, $Q = R(\pi^\tau)$.

Finally, if all parameters are privately observed, that is, $N^t \cap N^s = \varnothing$ for all $t \neq s \in T$, then $K = \Theta^T = \Theta$, and $F = Q$.   Q.E.D.

The intuition for this result is easily seen, at least when all parameters are observed privately. Consider the revelation game whose allocation rule is Q, and suppose the true value of the parameter vector is θ. If everyone else is telling the truth and agent t lies by reporting δ^t, then he receives the bundle given by evaluating Q at θ_k for components k which t does not observe and δ_k for components k which t does observe. The assumption that Q satisfies IC means, however, that t prefers the bundle given by evaluating Q at θ to the other bundle just described, that is, given that everyone else tells the truth, t prefers to tell the truth. In this case, the final allocation is simply Q. If t observes some parameters in common with other agents, then he can be made even worse off by lying about these if everyone else is telling the truth, because any discrepancy can be punished by giving everyone the worst possible allocation.

Given any achievable contingent allocation (i.e., one which is the equilibrium allocation of some mechanism), Theorem 5.5 states that this contingent allocation must satisfy IC. Theorem 5.6 then implies that the allocation can also be achieved as the truthful equilibrium of a revelation game. Therefore, Theorems 5.5 and 5.6 may be combined as

Theorem 5.7 (Revelation Principle) If Q is an equilibrium allocation of any mechanism, then there exists a revelation game R such that π^τ is an equilibrium strategy vector for R and $Q = R(\pi^\tau)$.

The importance of the Revelation Principle is that, if one is searching for optimal mechanisms, one can restrict one's search to revelation games. Since these are characterized by their allocation rules, this implies that one may conduct this search using ordinary mathematical programming techniques. In the following paragraphs, we define what we mean by "optimal mechanisms" and show how the Revelation Principle can be used to discover them.

To define optimality for mechanisms, we must first define preferences of agents over mechanisms. Since mechanisms may have multiple equilibria, we will define preferences over pairs $[M,(\mu,\pi)]$, where M is a mechanism and (μ,π) is an equilibrium for M.[9] Agent t *prefers* $[M,(\mu,\pi)]$ to $[M',(\mu',\pi')]$ if, for every $\theta^t \in \Theta^t$,

$$V_t[M(\pi),\theta^t] \geq V_t[M'(\pi'),\theta^t].$$

Strict preference is defined by a strict inequality for at least one θ^t. Note that this definition is based on "ex ante" expected utility, that is, on expectations taken with respect to information known before the start of the mechanism. The optimality definition that follows from this approach is called "ex ante optimality" by Holmstrom and Myerson (1983). The reader is referred to that paper for some other definitions. Note also that the definition of preference depends only on equilibrium allocations of mechanisms. Thus the cost of operating a mechanism is ignored.

A coalition $A \subset T$ can *block* $[M,(\mu,\pi)]$ if there is a mechanism M_A in which only agents in A participate and whose allocations are in $\lambda(A)$ with probability one such that, for some equilibrium (μ_A,π_A) of M_A and each $a \in A$, a prefers $[M_A, (\mu_A,\pi_A)]$ to $[M, (\mu,\pi)]$ with strict preference for at least one a. A mechanism M is a *core mechanism* if, for some equilibrium (μ,π) of M no coalition can block $[M, (\mu,\pi)]$; M is *Pareto optimal* if, for some equilibrium (μ,π), T cannot block $[M, (\mu,\pi)]$. The equilibrium referred to in the definition of core (or Pareto optimal) mechanism is called a *core (or Pareto optimal) equilibrium*.

We have the following general result that follows immediately from the Revelation Principle.

Theorem 5.8 If M is any core (Pareto optimal) mechanism and (μ,π) is any core (Pareto optimal) equilibrium for M, there exists a revelation game R such that R is a core (Pareto optimal) mechanism, π^τ is a core (Parto optimal) equilibrium strategy vector for R, and $M(\pi) = R(\pi^\tau)$.

Theorem 5.8 can be used to find core or Pareto optimal mechanisms in given environments. For example, for the employer–worker model discussed at the beginning of this section, consider the following program: choose $[y(\theta),r(\theta)]$ for $\theta \in \{a,b\}$ to maximize

$$\gamma_1\{p[y(a)-r(a)]+(1-p)[y(b)-r(b)]\}+\gamma_2\{r(a)-[y(a)/a]^2\}$$
$$+\gamma_3\{r(b)-[y(b)/b]^2\}$$

subject to (5.7), (5.8), and IR and Feasibility as previously defined, where the γ_i are arbitrary weights.[10] Suppose that $[y^*(\theta), r^*(\theta)]$ is a solution of this program. Then it is easy to see that the revelation game whose allocation rule puts probability one on $[y^*(\theta), r^*(\theta)]$, given θ, is a core mechanism. Moreover, as we vary the vector of weights γ, the solutions of this program represent *all* the core revelation games. Therefore, Theroem 5.8 implies that these solutions represent all the core equilibrium allocations of all core mechanisms.

EXERCISES

5.1. For the Leader–Follower example with $p > 0.5$, verify formally that the following is a sequential equilibrium: Leader always chooses "large," Follower infers nothing from Leader's choice, and Follower always chooses "large." (*Hint*: Use the sequence of strategies for Leader of always choosing "small" with probability $1/n$ and "large" with probability $1 - 1/n$ for $n = 1, 2, \ldots$, and the corresponding beliefs for Follower derived from Bayes' rule to justify the equilibrium assessment.)

5.2. Consider a market with one incumbent firm and one potential entrant. The costs of operating in this market may be high (with probability $1 - p$) or low (with probability p) depending on current technology, government regulation, and other factors. The incumbent firm knows whether costs are high or low, but the potential entrant knows only the above distribution. The incumbent moves first by setting a price for his output. This price can take on only one of two values, "high" or "low." The potential entrant then must decide whether to enter or stay out after observing the price charged by the incumbent. The potential entrant, if he decides not to enter neither gains nor loses, that is, his payoff is zero. If costs are high, the net payoff to the incumbent if he charges a high price and the potential entrant enters is zero, and the entrant loses 12. If there is no entry, the incumbent gains two. If, on the other hand, the incumbent charges a low price and there is entry, the incumbent loses one, and the entrant loses three. If there is no entry, the incumbent gains one. If costs are low, the incumbent charges a high price and there is entry, both the incumbent and the entrant gain two. If there is no entry, the incumbent gains four. If, on the other hand, the incumbent charges a low price and there is entry, the incumbent gains three and the entrant gains one. If there is no entry, however, the incumbent gains five.

  (a) Draw the extensive form for this game. Fill in all payoffs and other given information.
  (b) Find a sequential equilibrium and prove formally that it is one.
  (c) Is the equilibrium in (b) perfect?

Exercises 5.3–5.6 pertain to the following game.[11] There are two players called the firm and the market. The firm may be one of a finite set T of types. The firm knows its own type while the market knows only that the probabilities of the various types t are given by $\alpha(t)$ with $\alpha(t) > 0$ for each $t \in T$. The firm moves first, issuing a security denoted x from a finite set X of possible securities. The firm seeks to sell this security to the market in order to finance its operations. The market moves second, assigning a price $P(x)$ to the security issued. Denote the true worth to the market of a security x issued by a firm of type t by $W(x,t)$. Given the market's strategy, P, the firm cares only about the value of $P(x) - W(x,t)$, preferring larger values of this expression to smaller ones. The firm is also risk neutral. It may choose its security x randomly, that is, the firm's strategy is a conditional probability function $f(x \mid t)$ giving the probability of issuing security $x \in X$, given that its type is $t \in T$. The market is not an optimizing agent, but instead it assigns that price $P(x)$ to security x that is the expected worth of x given the market's posterior beliefs $\phi(t \mid x)$ about the firm's type t conditional on observing that the firm issued security x.

5.3. Carefully define a sequential equilibrium for this game, that is, give the conditions which f, P, and ϕ must satisfy. Pay special attention to defining ϕ when $f(x \mid t) = 0$ for all t.

5.4. For any sequential equilibrium (f, P, ϕ), prove that for any $x \in X$ and $t \in T$, if $f(x \mid t) > 0$, then $\phi(t \mid x) > 0$, and, conversely, if $\phi(t \mid x) > 0$ and $f(x \mid s) > 0$ for some $s \in T$, then $f(x \mid t) > 0$.

5.5. Suppose (f, P, ϕ) is a sequential equilibrium with the additional property that for any $x \in X$ and $t, s \in T$, if $f(x \mid s) > 0$ and $f(x \mid t) > 0$, then $W(x,t) = W(x,s)$. Also, for any x, let

$$M(x) = \min\{W(x,t) \mid t \in T\}.$$

Prove that, for any $x \in X$ and $t \in T$, if $\phi(t \mid x) > 0$, then $W(x,t) = M(x)$, and hence $P(x) = M(x)$.

Note that, under the above assumptions, $P(x)$ is the common value of $W(x,t)$ for any type t that would issue x, that is, any security issued, no matter what the true type of the firm, is correctly priced at its true worth by the market. Such equilibria will be referred to as *semi-revealing* since they reveal the true worth of the security issued but not necessarily the true type of the firm. Note that the description of the game only requires the market to price the security according to its ex post *expected* worth. The requirement that the equilibrium be semi-revealing is an extra restriction. This exercise asks you to prove that in any semi-revealing equilibrium, the true worth of the issued security must be the worth of that security if issued by a type of firm for which that security is worth less than for any other type of firm. In other words, in a semi-revealing equilibrium, the only type of firm that will issue a given security is a type that minimizes that security's value.

5.6. Let

$$X^*(t) = \left\{ x \in X \mid t \in \operatorname*{argmin}_{s \in T} W(x,s) \right\},$$

and assume

$$X^*(t) \neq \emptyset \quad \text{for every } t \in T. \tag{$*$}$$

Condition ($*$) states that, for each type of firm, there is at least one security such that that type of firm minimizes the worth of that security. Let $n(t)$ be the number of elements of $X^*(t)$. By ($*$), $n(t) > 0$ for each t. Let

$$f(x \mid t) = 1/n(t) \quad \text{if } x \in X^*(t),$$
$$= 0 \qquad \text{otherwise.}$$

This strategy simply picks at random a security for which the given type of firm is the worth minimizing type.

(a) Show that for any $x \in X$, $f(x \mid \tau(x)) > 0$, where $\tau(x)$ is any $t \in$ argmin$\{W(x,s) \mid s \in T\}$.
(b) Define ϕ and P by

$$\phi(t \mid x) = \frac{f(x \mid t)\alpha(t)}{\sum\limits_{s \in T} f(x \mid s)\alpha(s)},$$

$$P(x) = \sum\limits_{s \in T} W(x,t)\phi(t \mid x).$$

Note that ϕ is well-defined by part (a). Show that f previously defined, together with this P and ϕ, form a semi-revealing sequential equilibrium.
(c) Define a sequential equilibrium (f, P, ϕ) to be *fully revealing* if ϕ is degenerate for each x. Suppose that $X^*(t) \cap X^*(s) = \emptyset$ for $s \neq t$. Show that the foregoing f, P, and ϕ constitute a fully revealing equilibrium.

Exercises 5.7–5.11 pertain to the following model. There are three persons, two goods, and one period. The two goods are money and a Picasso painting. The three agents are called 0, 1, and 2; their preferences are given by

$$U_0(m,p,\theta) = m,$$
$$U_t(m,p,\theta) = m + \theta_t p \quad \text{for} \quad t = 1, 2,$$

where m is the money holding of the agent, p is an indicator of whether the agent possesses the painting ($p = 0$ indicates that he does not own it, $p = 1$ indicates that he does), and $\theta = (\theta_1, \theta_2)$ is a vector of reservation prices for the painting for agents 1 and 2. Agent 0 is called the "seller" and agents 1 and 2 are called "buyers." Before trade each buyer knows his own reservation price and that the reservation price of the other buyer, say t, is drawn from the finite set Φ_t using the distribution α_t. All other features of the environment are common knowledge. There is no production and the painting is indivisible. The seller owns the painting initially and has no money while each of the buyers has $\bar{m}$ units of money and no painting. Assume that $\bar{m} \geqslant \max \Theta_1 \cup \Theta_2$.

5.7. Define formally the set of feasible allocations $\lambda(T)$ for this environment, where $T = \{0,1,2\}$ is the set of traders.

5.8. Describe a revelation game for this environment. Assume that money must be allocated deterministically given the moves of the players, but the painting may be assigned randomly. Suppose the seller seeks a mechanism that maximizes his expected utility. Explain why he needs to consider only revelation games for which truth-telling is a Nash equilibrium.

5.9. Set up the maximization problem for the seller's mechanism design problem mentioned in the previous exercise. Continue to assume that money must be allocated deterministically. Also assume that

$$\Theta_t = \{\theta^1, \ldots, \theta^r\} \quad \text{for } t = 1, 2,$$

where $r > 1$, and $\theta^i < \theta^{i+1}$. Finally, assume that the buyers cannot be forced to play.

5.10. Show that the individual rationality (IR) constraint for buyer t and θ^i, $t = 1, 2$, $i > 1$, is implied by the IR constraint for θ^1 and the incentive-compatibility (IC) constraints.

5.11. Use the IC constraints to show that buyer t's probability of receiving the painting is increasing in his reservation price, while his expected money allocation is decreasing, for $t = 1, 2$.

NOTES

1. This subsection is based on Kreps and Wilson (1982).
2. The preceding discussion is based on Grossman and Perry (1986). For a related and somewhat weaker concept, see Cho and Kreps (1986).
3. The game analyzed at the beginning of this section (see Figure 5.1ff) is an example of the difficulty in defining beliefs sensibly when the strategy vector is not strictly positive.

4. This section is based primarily on Harris and Townsend (1981). See also Harris and Townsend (1984) and Myerson (1979).
5. Although this is the only reason in this example, it is possible to construct examples in which some FI-optimal allocations that do satisfy IC are not optimal in an "ex ante" sense to be defined later.
6. Little has been done to investigate the case in which such agreements are not enforceable. See Green and Laffont (1987) and Crampton (1984).
7. It has been suggested that, since the utility functions may depend on θ, one can solve this problem by redefining utility to be "minus infinity" for those values of (c, θ) for which c is not feasible given θ. This could make an otherwise well behaved utility function discontinuous thereby causing problems with the analysis. Moreover, I am not aware of any formal demonstration that this approach works.
8. The definition of "mechanisms" in Harris and Townsend (1981) is slightly different from that given in the text. In particular, in a Harris–Townsend mechanism each agent can observe all previous moves of other agents while this need not be the case in an extensive form game (by correctly specifying information sets). Also their equilibrium concept differs slightly from sequential equilibrium. Harris and Townsend do not allow for random strategies, and their specification of how beliefs are revised when a node is reached that has zero probability of occurring under the given strategies is different from the Kreps and Wilson (1982) specification. In Harris and Townsend, such beliefs are assumed to coincide with the initial beliefs instead of being limits of Bayesian beliefs corresponding to strictly positive strategies as described in Section 5.1. These changes do not affect the results in Harris and Townsend.
9. Harris and Townsend (1981) implicitly assumed that all mechanisms have unique equilibria. As a result, they defined preferences over mechanisms. The development that follows is, therefore a slight generalization of their results to situations in which mechanisms may have multiple equilibria.
10. An additional IR constraint is required, namely, the constraint that the employer prefers the allocation to $(0,0)$ in the ex ante sense, that is,

$$p[y(a) - r(a)] + (1 - p)[y(b) - r(b)] \geq 0.$$

11. This game is based on a model in Brennan and Kraus (1986).

REFERENCES

Brennan, M. and A. Kraus, "Efficient Financing Under Asymmetric Information," working paper, June 1986.

Cho, I-K. and D. Kreps, "Signalling Games and Stable Equilibria," working paper, Graduate School of Business, Stanford University, February 1986.

Crampton, P., "Sequential Bargaining Mechanisms," in "Two Papers on Sequential Bargaining," IMSSS Technical Report #444, Stanford University, 1984.

Green, J. and J-J. Laffont, "Posterior Implementability in a Two-Person Decision Problem," *Econometrica*, **55,** 1 (Jan. 1987), pp. 69–94.

Grossman, S. and M. Perry, "Perfect Sequential Equilibrium," *Journal of Economic Theory,* **39** (1986), pp. 97–119.

Harris, M. and R. M. Townsend, "Resource Allocation Under Asymmetric Information," *Econometrica,* **49,** 1 (Jan. 1981), pp. 33–64.

———— "Allocation Mechanisms, Asymmetric Information, and the 'Revelation Principle'," Chapter 11 in *Recent Advances in Microeconomics and Welfare,* George R. Feiwel (ed.) (New York: Macmillan, 1984).

Holmstrom, B. and R. Myerson, "Efficient and Durable Decision Rules with Incomplete Information," *Econometrica,* **51,** 6 (Nov. 1983), pp. 1799–1819.

Kreps, D. M. and R. Wilson, "Sequential Equilibrium," *Econometrica,* **50,** 4 (July 1982), pp. 863–894.

Myerson, R., "Incentive Compatibility and the Bargaining Problem," *Econometrica,* **47,** 1 (Jan. 1979), pp. 61–74.

Selten, R., "Spieltheoretische Behandlung eines Oligopolmodells mit Nachfrage-tragheit," *Zeitschrift fur die gesamte Staatswissenschaft,* **121** (1965), pp. 301–324.

———— "Re-examination of the Perfectness Concept for Equilibrium Points in Extensive Games," *International Journal of Game Theory,* **4** (1975), pp. 25–55.

Townsend, R. M., "Optimal Multiperiod Contracts and the Gain from Enduring Relationships Under Private Information," *Journal of Political Economy,* **90,** 6 (Dec. 1982), pp. 1166–1186.

Index

Action, 20–21, 23–24, 36–37. *See also* Decision
 space, 45
Allocation(s), 52–53, 55, 66, 117–22, 124–26, 130–31
 attainable, 52–54, 66, 86
 contingent, 117–20, 122–25
 equilibrium, 73, 83, 125–27
 full-information efficient, 118. *See also* FI; Full-information
 IC. *See* Allocation(s), incentive compatible
 incentive compatible, 118. *See also* IC; Incentive-compatibility
 parameter-contingent. *See* Allocation(s), contingent
 Pareto optimal. *See* Pareto, optimum
 rule(s), 122, 124–27
Assessment(s), 112–15
 consistent, 113–14
 equilibrium, 116, 127
Asset pricing, vii, 20

Back, Kerry, viii
Banach space, 4–6
Bayes' rule, 108–9, 113–14
Belief(s), 107–10, 112, 114–15, 121, 127, 130–31
 Bayesian, 109, 113, 131
 equilibrium, 108
 off-equilibrium-path, 109
 posterior, 107–8, 128
 prior, 107, 109, 119–20
 system(s) of, 112–13
Bellman's equation, 21
Benveniste, L. M., 13, 18

Berge, C., 10–12, 17–18
Bewley, T., 85, 87, 95, 104
Blackwell, D., 21–22, 48–49
Bond(s), 51, 65, 83
Borel
 set, 15–16, 20, 74, 77–78, 90
 sigma-algebra,15
Borucki, Lynda, viii
Bounded, 52, 61, 92
 function, 19–24, 26–27, 35, 46, 94, 98, 103
 linear functional, 7, 21
Brennan, M., 131
Brock, W. A., 78, 87
Budget constraint, 51, 53–54, 100–101, 103

Capital, 19, 27, 34–35, 39–40, 43, 45, 48–49, 52, 65–69, 71–73, 75–77, 80, 82–83, 89–90, 92–96, 98–103. *See also* Intertemporal Capital Asset Pricing Model
Capital Asset Pricing Model. *See* Intertemporal Capital Asset Pricing Model
Capp, Al, 85
Cass, D., 48–49
Cauchy sequence, 4, 5, 22, 24
Cauchy-Schwartz inequality, 17
Cho, I-K., 130–31
Coalition, 120, 126
Common knowledge, 116, 120–21, 130
Competitive equilibrium. *See* Equilibrium, competitive
Complete space, 22, 24, 103. *See also* Normed linear space, complete; Banach space
Consumer(s), 51–52, 54, 66–67, 72, 74–75, 83, 86–87, 89–90, 92–93, 96, 98–103
 representative, 92–93, 95, 98, 103

Consumption, 19–20, 35, 39–40, 43, 45, 48, 52–54, 63–65, 68–69, 71–73, 83, 89–90, 94, 97–103, 116, 120
  plan, 61
  set(s), 51–52, 54, 75, 83, 90, 96, 98, 120–21
  set, convexity of, 54
Contingent claims, 98–99, 102–3
Continuity, 3, 8, 76, 79, 92
Continuous, 24, 79, 91, 94, 103
  correspondence, 8, 10–13, 26, 38, 76, 91
  function, 11–13, 19, 26–27, 35, 37–41, 43–46, 68, 75–76, 82, 93, 98, 103
  linear functional, 8, 54, 61, 70, 81
Contraction mapping(s), 22–25, 49, 98, 103
  fixed point theorem, 24
Convex cone, 91
Correspondence, 20, 45, 90
Crampton, P., 131

Debreu, G., 17–18, 51, 58, 60, 85, 87
Decision, 20–21, 28. *See also* Action
  correspondence, 29
  rule, 21. *See also* Policy
Denardo, E. V., 23, 26, 28, 48–49
Depreciation, 19, 72–73, 83
Differentiability, 13, 14 (Fig. 1.6)
  of value function, 18, 39–41, 77
Differentiable, 40–41, 68, 73, 91, 94
Discount factor, 20, 28, 38, 46–47, 52, 90
Distance, 4
Dividend(s), 47–48, 96, 98
Dual space, 7–8
Dynamic, vii
  model(s), vii, 18, 19
  optimization, 19–20
  programming, vii, 13, 19–21, 27–28, 31, 35, 37, 45–47, 49, 76, 89, 92, 94

Equation of motion, 45, 92. *See also* Law of motion
Equilibrium
  allocation. *See* Allocation, equilibrium
  assessment, 127
  competitive, 45, 50, 68, 78, 89
  core, 126–27
  Nash, 110–11, 114, 130
  Pareto optimal, 126
  perfect, 109, 114–15, 127. *See also* Trembling hand perfect
  price(s), 62–65, 72–73, 83, 93, 95
  quasi-valuation, 58–59, 61, 64, 81–82

Recursive Competitive, vii, 66, 89, 93, 98, 104. *See also* RCE
  sequential, viii, 105, 107–10, 113–16, 127–29, 131–32
  strategy. *See* Strategy, equilibrium
  subgame perfect, 112, 114. *See also* Strategy, subgame perfect
  truthful, 122, 125
  valuation, vii, 45, 50–51, 54–55, 59–61, 64, 68–71, 81–82, 87, 89, 95, 98, 102–3
Equity, 95
Euclidean norm. *See* Norm, Euclidean
Euclidean space, 5, 7, 20, 62
Event(s), 14–16, 63, 82, 109, 120
  algebra of, 15
  discernible, 14, 62
Extensive form game(s). *See* Game(s), extensive form

FI, 119, 131. *See also* Full-information
Filtration, 16–17, 74, 90
  adapted to, 16–17
Firm(s), 52, 54, 66, 71–72, 74–75, 83, 86, 89–91, 93, 95–103, 105, 127–29
First-order conditions, 41, 44, 70, 77, 97, 100
Fixed point, 24–26, 43–44, 78
  theorem. *See* Contraction mapping(s), fixed point theorem
Fomin, S. V., 10, 18, 24, 49
Forward contract(s), 65
Free disposal, 57, 86
Full-information, 119. *See also* FI
Functional equation, 21, 97
Futures contract(s), 65

Game(s), 105, 106 (Table 5.1, Fig. 5.1), 107, 110–15, 122, 128
  extensive form, vii, 105, 114–15, 122, 127, 132
  revelation, 116, 118–19, 122–27, 130
  sequential, 105
  tree. *See* Tree
Green, J., 131
Grossman, S., 130, 132

Hahn-Banach extension theorem, 86
Hansen, Lars, viii, 87
Harris, Milton, 116, 123–24, 131–32
Harris, Miriam P., v
Hemi-continuous
  lower, 8. *See also* LHC

upper, 8, 27. *See also* UHC
Holmstrom, B., 126, 132

IC, 118–20, 123–25, 130–31. *See also* Incentive-compatibility
ICAPM, 95, 97. *See also* Intertemporal Capital Asset Pricing Model
Incentive-compatibility, 118, 122–23, 130, 132. *See also* IC
Indifference curve(s), 117
Individual-rationality, 119, 130. *See also* IR
Information, 16
    asymmetric, 105, 131–32
    private, 105, 116, 121, 132
    representation of, 3, 14, 62
    set(s), 106, 110, 112–13, 115
    structure, 16, 82, 120–21
Insurance, 102
Interest rate, 72
Interior, 56–57, 68, 77, 83, 86, 100
Intertemporal Capital Asset Pricing Model, 95. *See also* ICAPM
IR, 119, 127, 130–31. *See also* Individual-rationality

Justify(ies) (an assessment), 114, 116, 127

Kolmogorov, A. N., 10, 18, 24, 49
Koopmans, T. C., 48–49
Kraus, A., 131
Kreps, D. M., 105, 108, 111, 114–15, 130–32

L_∞ space, 49
L_p space, 6
Labor, 51–54, 83, 85–86, 89–90, 92, 118
Laffont, J-J., 131
Lagrange multiplier, 70–71, 100
Law of motion, 20–21, 28–30, 76, 93. *See also* Equation of motion
Levine, David, viii, 86
Lexicographic ordering, 56
LHC, 8–10, 13, 17–18. *See also* Hemi-continuous, lower
Linear
    form, 54, 58, 69, 86–87
    function, 6
    functional, 6–8, 17, 54. *See also* Continuous, linear functional
    space, 3, 86. *See also* Normed linear space
Lotus 1-2-3, 31. *See also* 1-2-3
Lotus Development Corporation, 49

Lucas, R. E., Jr., 60–61, 64, 85, 88, 95, 97–98, 103–4
Luenberger, D. G., 5–7, 17–18, 58, 86–87
ℓ_∞, 6–8, 87
ℓ_1, 7–8, 87
ℓ_p space, 5

Markov, 90
    chain, 28
    process, 20, 29, 47–48, 77, 89, 95
Martingale, 98, 104
Maximum Theorem, 11
Measurable, 16–17, 62–64, 74, 90
Measure
    probability, 62, 74
    space, 62, 90
Mechanism(s), 105, 116, 118, 122–23, 125–26, 130–32
    core, 126–27
    efficient, 105, 116
    optimal 126
    Pareto optimal, 126
Mehra, R., 89, 94–95, 104
Mirman, L. J., 78, 88
Myerson, R., 126, 131–32

Norm, 4, 7, 20–21, 49, 52
    essential supremum, 6, 49, 63
    Euclidean, 5, 17
    L_p, 6
    ℓ_p, 5
    sup, 5, 17, 39, 52
    topology, 54
Normed dual, 7
Normed linear space, 4, 5, 7–8, 60
    complete, 4. *See also* Banach space
Numerical solution, 28, 31

One-sector model, vii, 20, 34, 35 (Fig. 2.1), 44 (Fig. 2.3), 45, 48, 50, 64, 73, 78, 82, 84, 88
1-2-3-, 31, 48–49. *See also* Lotus 1-2-3
Optimal
    ex ante, 119, 126
    full-information. *See* FI; Full-information
    growth model, vii, 48–49, 88. *See also* One-sector model
    growth problem, 28, 34, 67
    Pareto. *See* Pareto
    path, 43, 46
    policy. *See* Policy
    value. *See* Value, optimal

Optimality equation, 21, 24–25, 30–31, 38, 41, 45–46, 67, 76–77, 92–94. *See also* Bellman's equation; Functional equation

Pareto
  optimal allocation. *See* Pareto, optimum
  optimal equilibrium. *See* Equilibrium, Pareto optimal
  optimal mechanism. *See* Mechanism(s), Pareto optimal
  optimality, 50, 54, 59, 66
  optimum, 50, 54–55, 58–59, 66, 87, 92–94, 96–98, 102–3
  problem, 82–84
Park, Jong, viii
Perry, M., 130, 132
Policy, 21, 24–26, 28, 37–40, 47–48, 76–77, 81, 84, 97, 103
Preference(s), 51–52, 66, 75, 82, 98
  convexity of, 55
Preordering, complete, 51
Prescott, Edward C., viii, 60–61, 64, 85, 88–89, 94–95, 104
Present value, 54
Price(s), 6, 28–29, 45–47, 50, 53–54, 63, 70, 72–73, 81–82, 86, 89, 92–93, 95–96, 101–3, 127–28, 130
  asset, 104. *See also* Intertemporal Capital Asset Pricing Model
  forward, 54
  representation, 50, 86
  sequence, 8, 80, 87
  share(s), 95, 98
  system, equilibrium. *See* Equilibrium, price(s)
  system(s), 7–8, 88, 99
  vector, 50
  vector, equilibrium. *See* Equilibrium, price(s)
Pricing
  function, 92–93
  scheme, 60–61
Producer, 51
Production, 52, 63–64, 120, 130
  plan(s), 61, 70, 93
  possibility set, 52, 65, 75, 83, 91, 95, 99, 120
  set, 51
Profit(s), 28, 54
  function, 53–54
  maximization, 70, 93, 96,103
Put option, 47–48

Ramsey, F. P., 48–49
Random variable, 16
RCE, 93–96, 98–99, 102–3. *See also* Equilibrium, Recursive Competitive
Recursive Competitive Equilibrium. *See* Equilibrium, Recursive Competitive
Rest-point, 43, 83–84. *See also* State(s), steady
Return function, 20, 28, 30, 45, 47
  optimal, 25
Returns to scale, 57, 91, 93
Revelation game. *See* Game(s), revelation
Revelation Principle, viii, 105, 116, 118, 125–26, 132
Richard, Scott, viii
Risk, 99, 128

Saturation point(s), 51, 55, 58, 61, 68, 80, 83–84
Scheinkman, J. A., 13, 18
Security, 128–29
Selten, R., 109, 111, 114, 132
Sequential equilibrium. *See* Equilibrium, sequential
Sequential rationality, 112 (Fig. 5.3). *See also* Sequentially rational
Sequentially rational, 112–14. *See also* Sequential rationality
Set-valued mapping, 8. *See also* Correspondence
Shanken, Jay, viii
Share(s), 47, 95–97. *See also* Price(s), share(s)
Shmoo, 52, 54
Sigma-algebra, 3, 15–17, 62, 74
Solow, R. M., 48–49
Spreadsheet, 31, 48–49
State(s), 20–21, 23, 29, 36–37, 46, 64, 82, 92–93, 99
  of nature, 73, 76, 99, 106
  space, 28, 30, 45
  steady, 43, 45–46, 72, 77–78, 84–85, 88. *See also* Rest-point
  of the system, 20–21
  of the world, 3, 6, 15, 50, 62, 75, 77
  variable(s), 29, 37, 47, 89, 92
Strategy(ies), 107, 110, 112–14, 124–25, 127–29, 131
  equilibrium, 108–9, 114, 122–26
  perturbed, 108–10, 114–15
  subgame perfect, 111
  vector(s), 110–14, 122–26, 130
Subform, 110, 112

Subgame(s), 110–12, 114
  perfect equilibrium. *See* Equilibrium,
    subgame perfect
Support Theorem, 58

Tax(es), 83–84
Threat(s), 111, 114
Townsend, R. M., 116, 122–24, 131–32
Transition
  function, 90, 95
  probability(ies), 90
Tree, 105, 110
Trembling hand perfect, 109, 114
Triangle inequality, 4, 25, 79
Truncated, 63–64
Truncation, 61, 64
Turnpike Theorem, 45

UHC, 8–13, 17–18. *See also* Hemi-continuous, upper

Utility function, 52, 65
  period, 34, 52, 74, 83, 90

Valuation
  equilibrium. *See* Equilibrium, valuation
  function, 60
  functional, 50
Value, 41
  of a commodity point, 54
  function, 3, 21, 28, 30, 46–47, 93, 96, 100
  optimal, 30, 38
  of an optimal policy, 34
Vector space, 3, 7, 18, 51. *See also* Linear,
  space

Wage, 54
Welfare economics, fundamental theorems
  of, 54, 94
Wilson, R., 105, 108, 111, 114–15, 130, 132

Zilcha, I., 78, 88